childstyle

Decorating Ideas & Projects For Kids' Rooms

Better Homes and Gardens® Books
Des Moines, Iowa

Better Homes and Gardens® Books
An imprint of Meredith® Books

ChildStyle Decorating Ideas
Editor: Amy Tincher-Durik
Contributing Editor and Project Writer: Amber D. Barz
Contributing Art Director: The Design Office of Jerry J. Rank
Copy Chief: Terri Fredrickson
Copy and Production Editor: Victoria Forlini
Editorial Operations Manager: Karen Schirm
Managers, Book Production: Pam Kvitne, Marjorie J. Schenkelberg, Rick von Holdt
Contributing Copy Editor: Jane Woychick
Contributing Proofreaders: Becky Danley, Beth Lastine, Erin McKay
Indexer: Kathleen Poole
Illustration: Burns Design
Electronic Production Coordinator: Paula Forest
Editorial and Design Assistants: Kaye Chabot, Karen McFadden, Mary Lee Gavin

Meredith® Books
Editor in Chief: Linda Raglan Cunningham
Design Director: Matt Strelecki
Executive Editor, Home Decorating and Design: Denise L. Caringer

Publisher: James D. Blume
Executive Director, Marketing: Jeffrey Myers
Executive Director, New Business Development: Todd M. Davis
Executive Director, Sales: Ken Zagor
Director, Operations: George A. Susral
Director, Production: Douglas M. Johnston
Business Director: Jim Leonard

Vice President and General Manager: Douglas J. Guendel

Better Homes and Gardens® Magazine
Editor in Chief: Karol DeWulf Nickell

Meredith Publishing Group
President, Publishing Group: Stephen M. Lacy
Vice President-Publishing Director: Bob Mate

Meredith Corporation
Chairman and Chief Executive Officer: William T. Kerr

Chairman of the Executive Committee: E. T. Meredith III

All of us at Better Homes and Gardens® Books are dedicated to providing you with
information and ideas to enhance your home. We welcome your comments and suggestions.
Write to us at: Better Homes and Gardens Books, Home Decorating and Design Editorial
Department, 1716 Locust St., Des Moines, IA 50309-3023.

If you would like to purchase any of our home decorating and design, cooking, crafts,
gardening, or home improvement books, check wherever quality books are sold.
Or visit us at: bhgbooks.com

contents

gettingstarted

Children's rooms are special spaces. They serve as havens for children, soothing retreats that envelop them with happiness at the beginning and end of each day. Unlike gathering areas, rooms shared by all family members, **children's quarters can be geared to their specific needs.**

Invest your decorating dollar with long-term growth in mind: **Plan and design beautiful, hardworking rooms that can grow and adapt with your child.** Whether you have a newborn, a school-age child, or both, **avoid age-specific products and design motifs that will require replacement** in only a year or two. To ensure a lasting decorating scheme, consider what your child's needs will be in five years and make selections that will meet his or her needs both now and then.

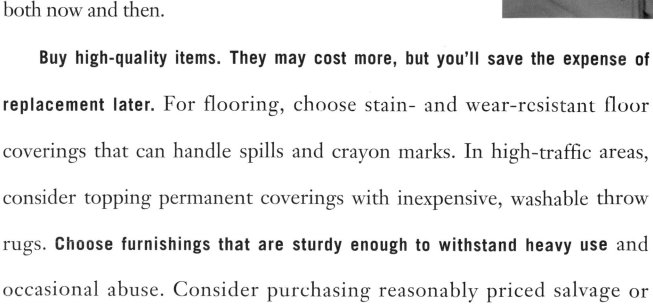

Buy high-quality items. They may cost more, but you'll save the expense of replacement later. For flooring, choose stain- and wear-resistant floor coverings that can handle spills and crayon marks. In high-traffic areas, consider topping permanent coverings with inexpensive, washable throw rugs. **Choose furnishings that are sturdy enough to withstand heavy use** and occasional abuse. Consider purchasing reasonably priced salvage or reproduction pieces that boast a timeworn look. These pieces won't be negatively affected by another scratch or two. For window treatments, upholstery, and bedding fabrics, pick classic over youthful; **select solids, stripes,**

checks, and small prints in cheerful colors. Sturdy, washable cottons or cotton blends are wise choices.

Select wall color and wallcoverings with care. Few people enjoy removing and replacing wallpaper; repainting is easy, but hiding drastic color choices may require multiple coats of paint. For added durability, choose washable paints or scrubbable wallcoverings that can survive a handprint or two.

If your child is old enough, involve him or her in motif, fabric, and color selections. Browse through the pages of this book together to see which looks appeal to you both. The first five information-packed chapters provide numerous examples of charming children's rooms **designed with longevity in mind.** The last chapter, beginning on page 108, offers **projects and smart techniques** to help you create the ideal room for your child. **Above all, enjoy the process.** Creating a safe, comfortable haven for your child is one of the many joys of parenthood.

rooms that grow

roomsthatgrow

Plan a nursery with the future in mind: Choose furnishings, fabrics, accessories, and surface treatments that can adapt as your child grows.

MIX AND MATCH. An eclectic mix of old and new furniture and accessories keeps the ambience in any child's room timeless and welcoming. In both the nursery and preschool variations of this bedroom, a mix of tag sale finds and heirloom pieces creates a comfortably worn look. Painting each piece of furniture and then distressing it by sanding the edges where natural wear occurs visually ties together the unrelated pieces. Gender-neutral yellow and white stripes serve as a soft nursery background that will look equally charming when the child reaches school age.

A leaf mobile hangs above the crib *opposite* to create the feeling of sleeping under a tree. When the child was old enough to climb, a full-size bed replaced the crib.

The nursery color scheme began with the full-size bedding *above right*, which originally adorned a guest bedroom. Slipcovers, shades, and bedding don't necessarily match, but the prints are complementary in scale. Sweet accessories, such as needlepoint pillows and sock monkeys, personalize the room.

For information on how to paint striped walls, see page 25.
For additional decorative painting instructions, see pages 110–112.

DESIGN A NURSERY TO GROW WITH YOUR CHILD

Select lasting colors. It's OK to stray from traditional blue or pink schemes. Gender-neutral colors, such as reds, greens, and yellows, can create a timeless look.

Avoid large doses of short-lived themes. If you are considering a novelty motif—such as the latest superhero or cartoon character—ask yourself if your child will outgrow it. If your answer is yes or maybe, incorporate a few low-cost changeable accessories that feature the motif, such as pictures and pillowcases.

Consider putting a bed in the nursery so you'll be comfortable on the nights when your baby needs extra attention. When the child grows, he or she can move to the bed, and you can remove the crib with little disruption.

●**CRIB SAFETY** All cribs made after 1992 meet current safety standards set by the U.S. Consumer Product Safety Commission. If you want to use a hand-me-down crib and are not sure of its age, check that the slats are no more than 2⅜ inches apart. Replace missing or cracked slats and broken hardware. Avoid cribs that have cutouts in the headboard or footboard and cribs with drop-side latches that a baby can easily release.
●**CRIB PLACEMENT** Place a crib far from draperies or blinds with loose cords, both of which can cause strangulation. Cribs placed in the center of the room are safest and present the baby as the focal point of the nursery.

PRIMARY FUTURE. Primary colors and vintage decorating schemes are ideal choices for children of all ages. Because bright colors are believed to be more readily distinguished by a newborn's developing eyes, pediatricians encourage exposure to contrasting colors, such as black and white or reds, yellows, and blues. These cheerful colors easily make the transition to toddler or teen decor. Traditional fabrics, including gingham checks and floral prints, are also good choices for decorating longevity: They never go out of style and are usually sophisticated enough to serve a child of any age.

As shown *above* and on pages 14 and 15, tan walls, primary blues and reds, and a nautical theme allow the room to change with the occupant. With the removal of one side rail, the crib converts into a child-size daybed. A step stool helps little ones climb in and out

bed. When the daybed becomes too small for your growing child, replace it with a __ze bed, which will work for sleepovers and last through the high school years.

Timeless styling and a honey-tone wood finish make the crib *opposite* versatile enough _ a newborn boy or girl.

Replace a crib with a bed when a child grows to 35 inches or shows an ability to _limb. The crib *above* converts into a toddler daybed when one of the side rails is removed. _o smooth the transition between crib and full-size bed, consider a convertible crib bed or _ake a simple plywood frame to hold the crib mattress a foot or two above the floor.

Primary Future continued on page 14

● **CHOOSING A CRIB** The crib you select may become a family heirloom. Think safety and quality when making your selection, and choose a finish that will look equally attractive for a boy or a girl. Consider a crib that converts into a toddler's daybed as shown *above*. The same linens fit the crib and the daybed, and the small bed size eases the eventual transition to a full-size bed.

Primary Future continued from page 13

    To make a primary color scheme suitable for a teen, emphasize the neutral tones of the room and consider black or navy as an accent. Work in one dark element—a rug or comforter, for instance—for a sophisticated touch.

● A classic red full-size bed replaces the toddler's bed *below*. A bulletin board and boat paddle serve as wall art, replacing the framed child-like prints. A more grown-up quilt, accented with red, white, and blue stars, replaces the crib bedding.

KNOB APPEAL

To customize any dresser, personalize the knobs. Let your child help you choose a motif. Consider floral, fruit, star, stripe, or polka-dot motifs. A simple design, such as the sailboats shown *below,* is best for the small surface. Purchase plain wooden knobs from a hardware or crafts store, choosing ones that fit on the same screws as the existing knobs. Sand, clean, and prime the knobs; let dry. Paint the knobs with a base coat of latex or acrylic paint in the desired color; let dry.

If painting freehand, practice drawing your design on a piece of paper. When you are satisfied with your picture, use a colored pencil to duplicate the design on the knob. If you prefer to stencil the design, either purchase ready-made stencils or make your own with clear acetate sheets.

After the drawing has been transferred to the knob or the stencil is in place, paint the design in latex or acrylic colors with a small artist's or stenciling brush. Seal with two coats of polyurethane.

● The chenille sailboat chair *above* is the perfect place for browsing picture books. In future years the chair can don a slipcover to serve another child with different color and motif tastes.

● The red painted dresser *right* is roomy enough to store diapers and baby clothes, as well as teen clothing. To update the dresser from baby to big boy, shiny black pulls replace white knobs adorned with hand-painted sailboats.

●**STORAGE TRUNKS** Inexpensive trunks, such as the one shown *left,* provide practical storage for older children: They are an ideal place to stash stuff when quick cleanup is required. Add a trunk at the end of the bed; use it to store toys and eventually sports gear, backpacks, or blankets. When closed, the top becomes a seat for getting dressed. Choose trunks with safety latches that will stand open at any angle and never slam shut.

●**THEME SCENE** Theme decorating makes choosing fabrics and accessories easy, but avoid trendy motifs. Choose themes that have lasted through generations so the room will not look too childish in a few years. Nautical, floral, fishing, and Americana motifs are a few examples of themes that stand the test of time. To appease a child who has specific theme or color tastes, add small, easily changeable doses of these favorites via accessories, such as inexpensive framed prints, throw pillows, rugs, or lampshades.

PINK PERFECTED. If you have your heart set on baby pink or blue, bala[...] your color choice with patterns and accessories that are appropriate for a c[...] of any age. Your room decor will last for a decade — or more — if you select t[...] right motifs.

● Feminine patterns, not baby prints, make the nursery *below* suitable f[...] transformation into a young girl's room. Floral tiebacks adorn the windows; a[...] pink and blue polka-dot cornice board tops off the windows in an attractive fashion. A full-size chair slipcovered in an oversize floral print makes late-nig[...] feedings comfortable for both adult and baby, and an upholstered ottoman doubles as a play table. A painted wooden step stool enables big sister or brother to peek in at the sleeping baby.

In the coordinated big sisters' room *above*, pink patterns are equally feminine and inviting and not in the least bit babyish. Colors and fabrics complement those used in the nursery, so accessories and furnishings can be shared and exchanged as needs and tastes change. Bed quilts are inexpensive and washable; the multihued pattern disguises stains. Inexpensive white tulle weaves through ring-shape tiebacks secured high on the wall. The tulle swag then ties around the bedposts to create a canopy look on each four-poster bed.

The bookcase *left* is securely bolted to the wall, keeping fragile objects safe up high and toys within reach. A simple ruffled skirt will convert the homework desk into a teenager's vanity.

●A PLACE TO SHARE If space allows, place an adult-size overstuffed chair or love seat in your child's bedroom. Make sharing the chair part of a nightly ritual, such as reading bedtime stories or sharing the events of each other's day.

BLUE PERFECTED. The soft blue nursery *above* readily converts to a school-age child's room, as shown *opposite top*. Three fabrics—a multicolor floral and two stripe patterns—add visual interest and ageless appeal. Using the window treatment as a guide, a furniture company custom-painted the twin bed *opposite top* and bureau *opposite right* to match.

● The white iron crib *above* works well for a boy or a girl. Forgoing a trendy look, the basic design ensures lasting style for future children.

● Painting the wooden bed frame blue *above* eliminates the need for a decorative bed skirt; however, while attractive, a bed skirt may be a better option if the child needs to store things under the bed.

● Wide drawers make the dresser *left* versatile enough to hold clothing for a child of any age. Framed photos above the dresser are an interesting alternative to a mirror.

●**VERSATILE BLUE** Who says baby blue is for little boys only? The soft, serene color works well for girls too. To make blue look more feminine, add a few floral prints.

●**WALLPAPER PICKS** Light-background wallcoverings make a room cheerful and bright. Choose scrubbable coverings that can withstand sticky fingers. White-background wallpapers accommodate changing wall art: Nail holes can be filled with white caulk so artwork can move from place to place.

PASTEL RAINBOW. Instead of choosing all pink for a little girl's room, consider using a rainbow of pastel colors. Then, as her tastes evolve, emphasize the colors she prefers and edit out those she dislikes.

In this girl's room, pink combines with yellow, mint green, lilac, and soft blue. The colors unite in a cheerful flower-shape throw rug. Classic calico bedding and striped drawer fronts impart style that will carry beyond the infant years.

The traditional-style, four-color four-poster convertible crib/daybed is suitable for a boy or girl; adjusting the colors will create a more feminine or masculine look. Changing finials adds personality; on the crib, birdhouse finials complement the nature theme suggested by framed butterfly wall art. Later, the finials can be changed to match your child's tastes or interests.

A timelessly styled, white louvered-door armoire provides extra storage, an ideal solution for homes with small closets. Initially baby clothes and supplies are stored here; the lower bins offer parents quick access. Later on the bins are perfect for stashing toys. Eventually the upper shelves of the armoire hold audiovisual equipment and books, and the bins stack to serve as a bedside table.

● With the removal of a side rail, the crib converts into a toddler's bed *below*. Yellow, pink, and white paint customize a simple changing table *left*. A diaper stacker tied to the armoire door pull keeps spares handy now and holds pajamas later on.

● The bedding used on the crib also fits the toddler's daybed. Throw pillows *below* replace crib bumpers, and a new table serves as a play center. Lamps and framed photographs replace the changing-table pad.

Pastel Rainbow continued on page 23

WINDOW TOPPER

Instead of using a traditional valance or cornice board, top your child's bedroom window with a simple open shelf. Measure the width of the window frame and purchase a ready-made shelf that either matches the measurement or extends several inches beyond the frame. Sand, prime, and paint or stain the shelf and brackets to match the window frame. Install support brackets so they align with the edges of the frame; this makes the shelf look as though it is actually part of the window. Top the brackets with the shelf and add trophies, toys, or other collectibles for display.

Pastel Rainbow continued from page 21

To transform a pastel-hued room into a preteen space, let your child choose the pastel colors she prefers, then use those colors in new accessories. Lavender and blue are the main colors for new bed linens *left;* a striped bed skirt makes the ensemble look mature.

On the wall, hang pictures of your preteen's choice; frame them to match the decor. Framed corkboard, covered with a complementary fabric and crisscrossed with ribbons, displays cards and pictures. Pastel painted frames that once held butterfly prints now show off favorite photographs.

● An attractive twin bed *left* takes up less space than a full-size bed, leaving more floor space for a desk chair and footstool.

● Originally a changing table, the painted dresser *below* holds everyday items, such as toiletries and a diary. Baskets organize hair accessories and jewelry.

●**FAIL-SAFE FABRICS** When choosing fabrics for your child's bedroom, opt for machine-washable geometrics, stripes, florals, and solids rather than animated characters he or she will quickly outgrow.

FAIL-SAFE WHITE. When white is used as a background color, its light-reflecting qualities make it a decorator's dream. To create a welcoming environment as in the nursery *above* and the school-age child's room *opposite*, pair white with as much texture and pattern as possible. Without a mix of texture and pattern, mostly white rooms can look sterile and uninviting.

⬤ Soft, cuddly chenille pampers a baby's skin. The fabric covers the dust ruffle and bumper pads on the crib *above*; chenille accents on the footstools and blankets pull the look together. Gauze netting suspended from the

ceiling adds an ethereal touch to the crib. Hung from a hook, the netting is easy to remove once the baby begins reaching upward. Textural chenille contrasts with the crisp white woodwork and soft striped walls. Adult-size furniture makes the room comfortable for grown-ups tending the baby. The pale blue-gray checked fabric runs diagonally on the chair cushions and footstool skirt and horizontally on the footstool top, providing visual variety. A square white cornice with a flounced checked valance underneath welcomes natural light.

An upholstered headboard, a bed skirt, and a tablecloth offer necessary pattern to the mostly white room *below*. Ragging pale peach paint over builder-white walls softens the background color and creates a canvas for a stenciled floral design. A complementary blue checked fabric accents pillows and the tabletop.

SOFT STRIPES

Wide wall stripes as shown *opposite* are soft, subtle, and easily re-created. First, paint the walls with a white base coat; let dry thoroughly. Using light blue chalk, measure and mark the walls at 6-inch increments. Use a carpenter's level and the chalk to mark a floor-to-ceiling dotted line, then mask off the marked lines with painter's tape. Using a sea sponge, fill in alternate stripes with blue paint, then carefully remove the painter's tape while the paint is still wet. For more decorative painting instructions, see pages 110–112.

INSTANT AGING White furniture works well in most children's rooms, but white finishes tend to show signs of wear easily. To make inevitable nicks and scratches less bothersome, consider making them a part of your plan. To give furnishings an instant timeworn appeal, use steel wool or sandpaper to rough edges and pulls.

the early years

theearlyyears

Whether you're expecting a newborn or raising a preschooler, this chapter will help you determine the perfect bedroom for your child.

BOLD DECISIONS. Send your baby's room to the top of the style charts with a hip color scheme that intrigues the eye and stimulates the imagination. For a contemporary look, select bold patterns and repeat the colors and motifs throughout the room, varying the scale for interest. Balance strong hues with strokes of white on the walls, furnishings, or fabrics. In this nursery, a bold mix of lime green and watermelon red provides a lively nurturing environment as well as a strong introduction to color.

Bright bedding fabrics served as the starting place for the color scheme here. Sporting all the patterns in the room, the hand-painted dresser makes a fun focal point. The polka-dot motif repeats on a colorful sidewall. Painted with giant dots, the wall treatment is an attention-grabber. Other fabric patterns are repeated on the reverse side of the bedding, on the window's custom-made wooden cornice, and on throw pillows and picture frames located throughout the room.

Suspended from the ceiling, a sheer polka-dot drapery *opposite* lifts the eye and adds a fanciful touch to this contemporary nursery. Other clever touches include a plywood cornice and an unfinished dresser that are painted to coordinate with the bedding fabrics.

Neutral carpeting and white walls, furniture, and accessories balance the bold green and red color scheme in this nursery.

For information on how to paint the dresser shown *above*, see page 122. For additional decorative painting instructions, see pages 110–112.

DRESS UP A DRESSER

To customize a dresser for your child's room, choose a piece of unfinished furniture. Sand the piece lightly and prime; let dry. Cover the dresser with two coats of latex enamel paint in the desired color; let dry. Using fabric or other motifs for inspiration, plan the patterns for the drawer fronts. On the dresser *opposite,* bedding designs were duplicated freehand with an artist's brush. For more control, mark off patterns such as stripes and checks with painter's tape or use stencils with acrylic or latex paints. Let your painted pattern dry thoroughly, then cover with two coats of polyurethane.

DRAPE A CRIB

For safety's sake, choose only lightweight, breathable fabrics and remove the drapery as soon as your child begins to reach or pull upward. To create an ethereal crib canopy, purchase a ready-made sheer scarf valance long enough to extend from floor to ceiling and back again (the scarf shown is 216 inches long). Tie a loose knot near the center of the scarf and attach it to the ceiling above the head of the crib using carpenter staples or cup hooks. Puddle excess fabric on the floor at opposite ends of the crib.

COUNTRY COMFORT. Invite comfort into your baby's space with a down-to-earth motif, as shown *left*. Calming blue walls and cheerful gingham checks combine with old-fashioned rag rugs and beaded-board wainscoting to produce a nursery filled with farmhouse charm.

To keep costs down and style high, recycled family furnishings and discarded items decorate the room. Homemade curtains, created from an old chenille bedspread and trimmed with a border cut from a sheet, add warmth and texture to the windows. Baskets, boxes, and peg racks keep clutter under control.

Square footage was limited in this second-story room, so play space was expanded into what was once under-the-eaves storage. A new doorway fitted with a swinging garden gate and a single step, shown on page 32, connects the two rooms. A twin bed was also added to the playroom; when the time comes, baby can move from crib to bed with little disruption in routine.

● A colorful, old-fashioned rag rug warms the whitewashed wood floors in the nursery *left*. Furnishings throughout the room—except the crib—are either hand-me-downs from relatives or flea market purchases.

● Tiny tennis shoes serve as clever tiebacks for curtain panels. The flowing panels were stitched from an old chenille bedspread and trimmed with contrasting fabric from an inexpensive sheet.

Country Comfort
continued on page 32

Country Comfort continued from page 31

● New wainscoting, purchased unfinished from a lumberyard, was primed and painted and then attached with finishing nails to the lower two-thirds of the nursery walls *opposite*.

● Open shelves and hanging rods flank the opening to the playroom *below*, providing storage for clothing and toys. A gingham curtain serves as a closet door.

● A homemade fabric-covered bulletin board *left* organizes birth announcements and birthday cards from future playmates.

●**WITHIN REACH** Give your child instant independence by keeping toys and books where he or she can reach them without any help. Even a crawler can head to a basket of favorite toys on the floor.

●**MIRROR ME** To give an extra dose of self-esteem to your baby, invite him or her to look in a mirror. Put the mirror in a spot where your baby can readily see it. In the room *opposite*, the mirror hangs directly behind the wicker chair where the baby is often held and rocked.

GINGHAM BULLETIN BOARD

Show off sentimental keepsakes on a custom-made bulletin board. Cover a piece of lightweight corkboard with a favorite fabric; adhere with hot glue. For a framelike finish, trim the fabric-covered board with rickrack. Attach picture hangers to the back of the board and hang the finished board in a prominent place to display birth announcements, birthday cards, and favorite drawings or photos.

PAINTED PARADISE. Meld traditional fabrics in soft, feminine florals with finely detailed furnishings to design a toddler's room pretty enough for a princess. The attractive harlequin diamond pattern on the wall *below* takes only a few hours to paint and sets the stage for upscale decorating—transforming the walls into the pages of a fairy tale.

In this toddler's room, coordinating pink floral and plaid fabrics define the overall color scheme. A meeting between the mural artist and the 3-year-old resident of the room narrowed down the mural theme to a fantasy-inspired faux bed crown, treasure chest, and trompe l'oeil arched windows. If you prefer working with fabric instead of paint, mount a three-dimensional bed crown behind the headboard and drape complementary fabrics from the crown.

● A faux-painted bed crown and cascading curtains adorn the wall behind the bed *left*. Faux swags decorate painted-on crown molding. A make-believe treasure chest rests on the trompe l'oeil window ledge.

● Intricate details such as faux-painted tiebacks *right* complete the fantasy.

● Storage drawers and a cozy window seat *below* fill previously underutilized space below a real window. The floral valance is sophisticated enough to appeal throughout childhood.

For decorative painting instructions, see pages 110–112.

●**HIRE A PRO** Unless you are an artist yourself, you will need to hire a faux-painting expert or mural artist to paint a sophisticated trompe l'oeil (fool the eye) mural on your walls. To find an artist in your area, contact local interior designers and art studios and ask for recommendations. Your local high school art instructor may also be able to recommend colleagues or students capable of mural design. When meeting with artists, ask to see portfolios or examples of their work and check references. If hiring someone to do the work for you is cost-prohibitive, look for trompe l'oeil wallcoverings that replicate everything from clouds to logs.

FRENCH TWIST. Coloring-book graphics and words written in two languages translate into kid-captivating fun and fantasy. Sherbet colors adorn the walls and furnishings and flow onto the floor by way of a blueberry-tone carpet.

A wide hand-painted border covers the lower third of the nursery walls where French and English words point to drawings of ice skates, clowns, and rubber duckies. The images were drawn on tracing paper, cut out, and traced onto the wall. Each motif was outlined with black latex paint and then filled in with various colors. Next, French and English identifiers were written, and finally, blue paint was applied for the background. Similar paint techniques upgrade an old armoire and unfinished dresser to folk art status, bringing the pieces into the overall scheme with harmonious hues and kid-friendly motifs. Dry-brushed yellow stripes on a white background provide

visual relief from the busy border.

● Carefree hearts centered on the drawer fronts, along with new pink painted bun feet, transform the simple dresser *above* into a decorative focal point.

● Similarly, wooden balls and bun feet purchased from a hardware store jazz up the old armoire *opposite* and visually connect it to the dresser. The scalloped top edge of the armoire is made out of plywood.

● The hand-painted border *left* enlivens the room and serves as a teaching tool for introducing a second language.

For information on painting stripes, see page 25.

●**UNIFY FURNITURE** To make unrelated pieces appear uniform and custom-made, add similar design elements to each piece. For example, add picture-frame molding to armoire and dresser drawer fronts and sides to create the look of recessed panels. Paint the newly created panels a different color for a one-of-a-kind look.

LIVING IN THE FAST LANE. Young racing enthusiasts will enjoy starting and finishing their day in this action-packed room. Racetracks loop across the floor and run down the bed linens. The bed, featuring carved head- and footboards painted to look like the blue ribbons at the start and finish lines of the track, can be repainted as the child grows. Attached to the top of the bedposts are blue and white checked flags, wired to look as though they are waving in the breeze.

The blue checked pattern flows across the comforter, separating the lanes of car-racing mice. The pattern also speeds around the room in the form of a painted border near the ceiling line. The floor features 2-foot-square painted checks and a superimposed racetrack—a valid excuse for leaving die-cast cars on the floor.

Horizontal brushstrokes in shades of yellow bring movement to the walls and are a complementary backdrop to the other design elements. Car-shaped cornices are made from hand-painted lightweight foam-core board.

● Lively movement courses through this bedroom. The dashed stripes on the bed linens *left* resemble passing lanes on a highway.

Brightly painted walls and race-motif fabrics transform the room *above* into a race car enthusiast's dream. The easy-to-paint toy car track that loops around the room turns floor space into play space. **For instructions on how to add a painted racetrack to a room, see page 118. Wall painting techniques are discussed on pages 110–112.**

●**GO FOR IT** When planning a baby's or preschooler's room, let your creativity flow. If you focus your creative energies on fabric and paint, a decorative redo is as affordable as repainting the walls and furnishings and replacing the linens. A coat of fresh paint and new bedding and window treatments will generate a completely different look.

●**VISUAL TRICKS** Fix architectural oddities with simple eye-fooling remedies. If a ceiling seems too high, add chair-rail molding to the wall 8 or 9 feet above the floor and paint the area above the molding a darker shade than the portion below. Or fill the top of the wall with an extra-wide border or stenciled design, as shown *above* and *opposite*.

ARTFULLY CRAFTED ALPHABET. From top to bottom, flexible styling makes this room comfortable for a baby now and an older child later.

Time-tested Arts and Crafts styling complements the decor in the rest of the house and makes the nursery appear as though it has always been there. When the fence-motif crib *left* gives way to a bed, accessories and style-conscious pieces will remain, including the under-window radiator cover *below* with cutouts that foreshadow the slats on the bed. A patterned black rug—a folk art classic—anchors the Craftsman-era theme. A black painted rocker and pierced-copper wall sconces keep the dark rug from looking too heavy in the large space.

The alphabet border appears permanent, but it's as flexible as the rest of the design. Hand-painted on hardboard panels, the border rests between the crown molding and the chair-rail molding. Every few feet, trim nails hold the panels in place. Depending on the ceiling height, attach the panels up high, as in this room, or mount the panels on the lower portion of the walls. These temporary effects are especially great if you live in a rental: When you move, you can take the panels with you. When the child outgrows the alphabet motif, remove the panels and replace them with a more mature scheme.

● Black, a color often used by Craftsman-era artisans, gives the room *below* and *opposite* long-lasting style.

● The large-pattern rug *below* balances the small floral print used on the chair cushions and crib bedding. The creamy whites of the crib and dresser and the soft green on the walls repeat in the black rug. The oversize alphabet border visually lowers the high ceiling.

ABSTRACT IMPRESSIONS. A diamond pattern, hand-painted on the walls, served as the starting point for decorating this decidedly different nursery. The pattern climbs to the top of the dormer wall to connect with perfectly painted cumulus clouds and a stylized wave motif that borders the room at the ceiling line.

A sheer diamond-pattern canopy shirred on a suspended rod crowns the crib, drawing attention to the clouds and the pitched ceiling. The canopy curtain, crib, and linens are white, so there is no chance of patterns clashing against the walls or furnishings. The other furnishings are intricately painted with an unusual combination of patterns.

The hues in the room range from pinks and blues to greens and golds, so almost any color can be accommodated in this space. Lighthearted enough for a baby's room, the painted pieces will look equally attractive in an older child's room or even a guest room. If your child's tastes evolve in an entirely different direction, the artfully painted pieces could also be relegated to a dining area or sunroom.

● An unusual mix of geometric patterns and a rainbow of colors offer the traditional nursery *below* an eclectic edge. Painted checks, diamonds, and botanical motifs adorn the dresser, rocker, and mirror.

● The diamond pattern of the canopy *opposite* echoes the hand-painted wall pattern. Solid-white bumper pads, sheets, and crib skirting harmonize with the canopy and painted ceiling treatment.

●**FLAUNT IT** If your child's room has some particularly attractive architectural elements, feature them as decorative focal points. For example, add emphasis to round-top windows by stenciling a colorful design around the arch. Show off a tray ceiling by surrounding it with a wallpaper border or by painting the top of the tray with a contrasting color. In this nursery, a bed canopy and cloud-painted dormer *opposite* draw attention to the interesting ceiling angles.

CRIB CANOPIES

Choose only lightweight, breathable fabrics for crib canopies and remove the drapery as soon as your child begins to reach or pull upward. The crib canopy in this nursery mounts to the ceiling differently than those featured on pages 24, 29, and 40. To secure a bed canopy in this fashion, first sew a simple rod pocket into the center of a scarf valance. Ready-made scarves come in lengths up to 216 inches, but high ceilings may require you to sew scarves together or to have one custom-made. Shirr the valance onto the decorative rod as you would any curtain. Suspend the curtain-clad rod from the ceiling with standard rod hooks that have been securely mounted with screws to the ceiling beam.

THREE-DIMENSIONAL DREAMS. Jump-start your toddler's imagination by creating a room that is as magical as anything make-believe. Playhouses ignite the imaginations of boys and girls alike. In the three rooms featured on pages 44 through 49, toddler-size playhouses harboring twin-size beds and ordinary materials—paint, fabrics, and furnishings—bring fantasies to life.

Here, a Scottish castle served as the inspiration behind the bed-and-playhouse combo. With bunk beds, secret hiding places, and a book nook in the ladder-accessed turret, the custom-designed castle offers tykes hours of enchanting play. Fashioned from stone-look laminate, the castle has no back walls, so mattresses, box springs, and bed frames can be moved in and out without being disassembled. A marvelous wall mural depicting scenes of Edinburgh Castle and Loch Ness (note Nessie's tail below the

window *above left*) surrounds the castle. On the wall opposite the bed, faux-painted stones border a trompe l'oeil window that features a view of the Scottish Highlands and a big-as-life Highland bovine. The real bench seat lifts to provide toy storage.

● Although the bed-and-playhouse combination *above left* is not much wider than a standard twin bed, the wall mural behind it makes the castle appear larger than life. Inside the turret, a sturdy ladder leads to the second bunk and a reading nook. A yellow and blue fabric inset creates castle detailing on the cornice above the custom-made denim-blue Roman shade.

● Gothic influences appear on the chair backs and the base of the tot-size table *above right*. Durable, easy-care neutral carpeting and a rocking chair comfy enough for both parent and child ground the room in reality.

● **MURAL MAGIC** If your plans call for something less elaborate than a three-dimensional castle, consider indulging your child's fantasies with a wall mural that encompasses the entire room. If painting a mural sounds like a project you might like to tackle, head to your favorite crafts store. Some larger stores stock stenciling kits that can help you create the look of a custom wall mural. Motifs range from Peter Rabbit-inspired gardens to sports arenas. See page 35 for tips on finding a professional muralist.

A DOLL IN HER HOUSE. This giant dollhouse houses bunk beds. The lower bunk sits right inside the front door, and occupants of the upper bunk can peek over the roof. The structure has no back wall; placing it in front of a window allows daylight to brighten the interior, but necessitates safety bars that cover the glass. Sturdy wooden shades add further protection from the glass and help control daylight.

Real siding, scalloped shingles, and fretwork grace the house facade. Swinging shutters attached to the front window openings are discards from the main house. The miniature recessed-panel door is fashioned from wood trim applied to plywood.

The window boxes and porch railing are
also made from common lumber. A round
drawer pull with a brass plate is the
perfect child-size doorknob. Silk flowers
and vines stand in for landscaping.

● Built in four pieces and then placed
on a wooden frame, the playhouse-bed
structure *opposite* makes double use
of a single space.

● Visitors who step onto the wood-slat
front porch *left* can press a doorbell that
plays 30 tunes. The miniature house also
features indoor and outdoor lighting.

● Inspired by the tulips on the quilt,
a custom-made stenciled design
decorates the stairs leading to the top
bunk *above*.

ALL FIRED UP. If you live with a firefighter wannabe, this bedroom design may be exactly what you're looking for. Fire-fighting play meets three-dimensional reality: a "truck" wall unit that provides a carpeted play area up top, a cozy sleeping area below, and plenty of storage space adjacent to the bed.

Each element of the room displays a fire-fighting theme while also serving a practical purpose. The closet is disguised as a set of lockers. The "First Aid" end of the truck provides armoirelike storage shelves behind the painted doors; "Dispatch Central" offers work and display space. The spots of the dalmatian mascot create a lively background on the walls and ceiling.

● The convincing details on the fire truck *above* include gauges, nozzles, and a coiled water hose. Covered with yellow laminate, the truck is durable enough to withstand roughhousing.

● Wide shelves *opposite top left* provide storage for toys, towels, and games. Drawers below the doors hold undergarments and socks.

● The closet *opposite top right* is disguised as lockers.

● White laminate covers the exterior surfaces of the desk *right*. For contrast, open cubbies are painted black on the inside. A leather-topped window seat makes a comfy reading spot.

●LONG-LASTING LAMINATES

Furnishings covered with laminates can be created in scores of colors to carry out virtually any theme. Durable and washable, the finish may scratch or chip if overly abused, but it never splinters.

To find a craftsperson capable of building a three-dimensional project like this wall unit, contact local interior design professionals and ask for recommendations. Trim carpenters, custom furniture makers, and cabinetmakers can design and construct projects of this magnitude.

Make Time for FUN

elementary
solutions

elementarysolutions

To let your child have a say in the decorating decisions for his or her room, browse these pages together for themes you can both live with.

HIP AND SQUARE. Flower-topped plaid panels on the walls give this elementary-age student's room one-of-a-kind design flair. Inspired by European design, the painted plaid looks like a fabric wallcovering and complements the freshly painted tag sale bed and dresser.

The plaid is achieved with 6-inch-wide vertical stripes of blue, orange, and burgundy that are crisscrossed with horizontal rows of peach, green, burgundy, and blue. The base coat is periwinkle. Pretty sprays of hand-painted flowers and butterflies create soft arches to relax the defined lines of the plaid.

Floral patterns and solid cotton chintzes and chenilles combine with a cotton brocade to give the bed texture and color. Periwinkle accents and painted floral sprays dress up the bed, night table, and dresser; plaid painted drawer fronts on the dresser complete the ensemble. A simple rag rug in complementary pastels warms the oak plank floor.

● Painted panels behind the bed and dresser showcase the main furniture in this little girl's room *right*. Hand-painted floral sprays soften the linear design. Stenciled flowers and leaves would create a similar look.

For decorative painting instructions for plaid wall panels, see page 123.

HIP WITH A HOP. Frolicking frogs, blades of grass, and a stretch of white picket fence set a playful mood in this spirited room. A fun green and blue frog fabric initiated the design theme, but to prevent its busy look from overtaking the room, the fabric is limited to a pile of throw pillows. This limited-use decorating technique works well for any busy fabric and for expensive decorator fabrics.

For extra interest, the frog pattern leaps onto the walls via paint and stencils. Placed randomly above the chair rail, the frogs break up the otherwise stark white upper walls. The emerald hue painted below the chair rail grounds the design.

Complementary solids and plaids dress up the bed, windows, desk, and bedside table. Overstuffed pillows on the bed front a picket-fence headboard; the pine pickets were sanded, primed, painted, and screwed to the bed frame. A reversible duvet cover, sewn in emerald and sapphire plaid, covers the bed. A window seat topped with a plump cushion and piles of pillows makes an inviting spot for reading or window gazing.

● Dressmaker details, such as piping, pleats, and buttonhole edging, give the furnishings *left* a tailored look.

● Stenciled grass seems to grow out of the chair rail *below*.

For instructions on upholstering a piece of wooden furniture such as the desk *below*, see page 123.

WHIT WITH WINGS. An insect-pattern bedding fabric served as the inspiration for this room. Design spunk comes from lively painted walls and colorful, easy-to-stencil embellishments on the furnishings. Winged creatures cut from brightly colored fabric scraps flutter atop windows dressed with white wood blinds. Orange paint and bug-shape knobs update a modest dresser; giant hand-painted flowers bloom above it.

Suspended from the ceiling, reading lights hide beneath mini canopies sewn from cheesecloth. To avoid a fire hazard, choose fire retardant fabric for the canopies and use lampshades that are wide enough to prevent contact between the bulbs and fabric.

● Bright colors and an adorable insect motif give the room *above* a decorative buzz. When the occupants are older, changing the window valances and bed linens will create a more sophisticated look.

● Orange paint and colorful insect-shape knobs give a simple dresser *opposite top left* design kick. Floral picture frames and bug-shape toys complement the nature scheme.

● Stenciled-on ladybugs as shown on the handmade doorknob pillow *opposite top right* and on the bedframe *opposite bottom* are sprinkled throughout the room.
For dresser painting advice, see page 29. For advice on covering a lampshade, see page 118.

●**CHOOSING THE RIGHT THEME** To pull off a themed scheme in your child's room, begin with a motif that will last longer than a movie run. Temper the design scheme by limiting the number of patterned fabrics to three or four and use white or another neutral to calm bright tones. Pick a favorite fabric, painting, or print as a starting point, then add coordinating elements. Sprinkle the motif on a variety of surfaces, from walls to lampshades.

Most school-age children enjoy participating in decorating decisions. To include your child in the design process, bring home several fabric samples you like and let your child choose his or her favorites from your pre-edited selections. If he or she insists on adding a trendy character print, look for sheets or pillowcases that feature the motif; then pair the linens with a coordinating solid-color comforter. Use throw pillows, picture frames, toys, and other accessories to carry out the theme.

For an elementary-age child, choose furniture that's classic enough to suit future needs and decorating schemes. Add colorful flourishes by painting bedposts or installing new hardware or handles to dressers and chests; making hardware replacements or repainting in a few years will create a fresh new look.

BLUE-RIBBON DESIGN. Considered hair necessities for many little girls, ribbons and bows served as the design inspiration for this bedroom. A blue and white bow-motif fabric used for the table skirt defines the predominate color palette. A complementary two-tone plaid adds more color and pattern. The washable wallcovering lends subtle pattern to the backdrop. White woodwork and trim moldings prevent the bright wall color from overpowering the small room.

Fabric patterns were selected with maturity in mind. Framed hot-air balloon prints, as well as toys and books, add color and decorative interest while revealing the tastes of the kindergartner who resides here. As she matures, accessories can be updated to reflect new interests, activities, or hobbies.

● Blue tones unite four different patterns in this girl's room *right*. Bows on the valance, duvet, and table skirt play up the ribbon-and-bow accent fabric without overdoing it.

● A wide tailored valance *below* shows off a large-scale plaid fabric selected to coordinate with the duvet fabric. The playful laced bow detail ties in with the pillow sham and table covering.
For wallpapering instructions, see pages 113–115. For window treatment instructions, see page 119.

●**MIX AND MATCH** To blend multiple patterns, choose patterns of different sizes and use color as a unifying factor. Limit the number of patterns to three or four, applying the busiest pattern in limited amounts. Temper strong patterns with solid colors. If in doubt, check out ready-mixed collections of coordinated fabrics.

NOW AND THEN. New office components blend with antique finishes to build a room that gracefully bridges the generations. Antiques can work well in a child's room; they have already withstood decades of use and they bring a sense of history and tradition to a newly decorated space. In this retreat designed for a boy, an antique mahogany sleigh bed, a mahogany dresser, and an old pine cupboard link the 11-year-old's lair to the rest of the antiques-filled home.

At almost 11 feet wide, the pine cupboard supplies generous behind-door storage for games and toys; open shelves harbor books and an aquarium. The deep dresser drawers accommodate stacks of T-shirts, shorts, and jeans. Maple wood stain ties the brand-new office desk and credenza top to the antiques. The new furniture provides the work area required by a computer-savvy kid. Apricot walls—a toned-down version of the preteen's request for orange—play up the warm wood tones. A tailored window valance picks up the wall color, the ruddy hues of the mahogany, and the blue of the bed linens. Teal-green paint connects the woodwork and door to the painted computer center.

● Family heirlooms mix with auction-house finds *left* and new, painted pieces *above* to create a decor masculine enough to meet the needs of a boy as he grows into a young man. Richly colored fabrics include blue denim, earthy plaid, ticking stripes, and a Native American print.

● Teal-green paint contrasts with the apricot painted walls *above* and links the new furnishings to existing woodwork.

●**WOOD-WISE** Mixing wood species can give a room more texture, color, and visual interest. Also consider a mix of stained and painted woods.

PAINTING FURNITURE
Unfinished furniture is often affordably priced—and easy to customize. Look for ready-to-finish pieces at home centers or at shops that specialize in unfinished furniture. Remove any drawers or exposed hardware, sand the piece lightly, prime, and let dry. Cover all the surfaces with two coats of durable latex enamel paint; let dry. To protect the surface, seal the piece with a coat of polyurethane. To complement the piece, paint window and door trims to match, using the same sanding, priming, and painting process. For more furniture-finishing ideas, see pages 15, 29, and 121–123.

PRETTY AND PASTEL. Defined by the pastel palette used throughout the home, this room cheerfully welcomes an elementary-age girl. The full-size bed is ample for one and comfy enough for overnights with a friend or sister.

Soft peach hues visually connect three fabric patterns: a blue-background floral, a simple peach and white check, and a lively multitone plaid. The sophisticated patterns combine with the friendly colors to make the ambience appealing for the child now and mature enough to please her as she grows older.

A classic mirror-topped dresser provides ample storage and display space and can double as a makeup vanity later. A desk is hand-painted to match the plaid pillow shams and bed skirt. Dragonflies stenciled on the white wooden chair seats and embroidered on the sheer white curtain panels add a touch of fun. Whitewashed floors are coated with polyurethane, making cleanup after art time a breeze.

● The curved white wooden bed and matching dresser in the little girl's room *right* will meet her needs from now until adulthood. Floral valances and bed linens are feminine and ageless.

● A small desk *below* suits a young child's homework needs. The table can easily be replaced with a full-size desk or computer armoire later.

For furniture customizing ideas, see pages 15, 29, and 121–123.

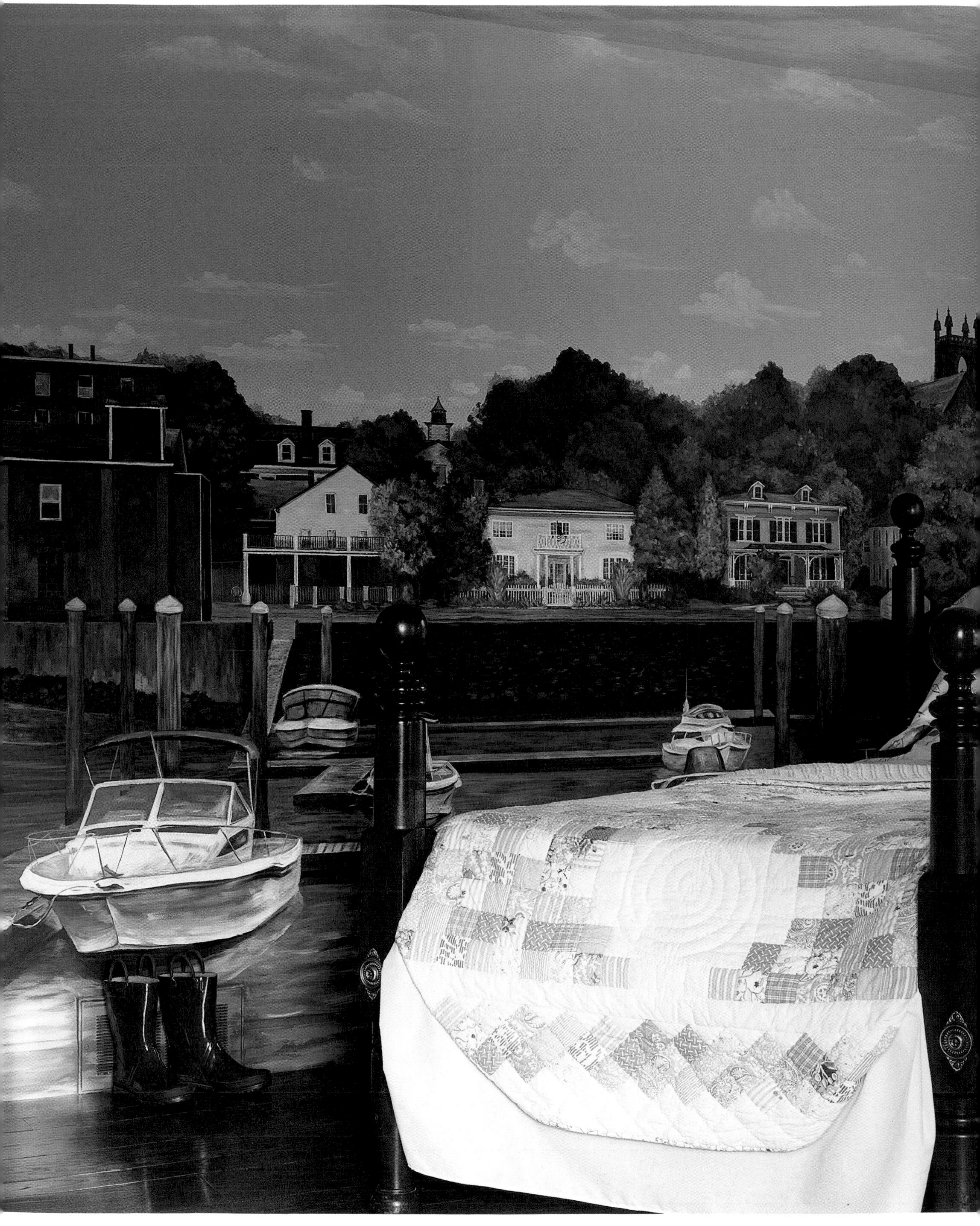

WALLS OF WONDER. An artfully painted wall mural fosters imagination without looking too age-specific. Because the lifelike harbor scene is colorful and detailed, furnishings and accessories are purposely kept simple.

Angled out from a corner of the room, an antique mahogany four-poster bed seemingly floats on the water in a tranquil bay. A simple patchwork quilt mimics the colors displayed on a nearby trompe l'oeil speedboat. Beside the bed, a delightful lamp has an actual buoy for a base and a shade covered in nautical maps. The wood plank floor resembles a wooden boat dock.

To create a sandbar-theme reading nook, canvas sailcloth panels replace bifold closet doors. Open shelves that run down one side of the niche are now conveniently filled with books. The top half of the closet, hidden behind the sail-like panels, retains its original function of storing clothing. The wall mural on either side of the closet depicts a marshy section of the bay. The interior of the closet displays a low, deep-colored border of painted sea grass. Sand-color carpet, shaped like a sandbar, spills out from the faux grass, creating an island of softness adjacent to the wood-plank floor. Fish, sailboats, and stripes decorate square pillows that invite island stopovers; it's a perfect spot for reading, dreaming, or hanging out with friends. Off the carpet sandbar, hand-painted fish swim across the floor, adding a playful touch.

● A painted mural depicting a serene harbor *left* encourages imaginative play in this young boy's bedroom. The tranquil image also creates an ideal resting spot.

● The carpet island *above* doubles as a play space and closet and continues the bay theme. Stock shelving units hold books, games, and sports gear. A roll-up window adds interest to the sailcloth curtain panel.

BLUE SKIES AHEAD. The zany design of this bedroom facilitates smiles and encourages children to engage in their favorite activities. Four separate activity centers—a write and think station, sleep and dream chamber, create and play area, and read and relax haven—stand ready to serve the occupant.

A funky hand-painted orange and green plaid desk, featured on page 68, anchors the think station.

Carrot shapes and faux-painted stepping-stones decorate the desk chair. The wire mesh bulletin board is an old garden gate spray-painted scarlet.

Next to the bed, a large sunflower reading lamp and the overgrown sunflower garden facilitate dreaming big. The picket fence and flowers also serve a second purpose: They disguise a radiator and window air-conditioning unit.

Purposely imperfect shingles top a barnlike display of toys. A roomy play table sports a checkerboard, good for both checkers and chess.

The read and relax haven, shown on page 69, is an inviting bay window seat painted to resemble a tree house. Flanked with hand-painted branches and leaves and filled with comfy overstuffed pillows, the recessed area provides a quiet getaway spot. An overhead sign guards against intruders.

Bright colors featured throughout the room are joyous, loud, and brassy enough to make a child's eyes grow large. Clouds dot sky-blue walls and ceiling and stylized painted grass serves as wainscoting. The dark-stained wood floor anchors the space and keeps the focus on the festive furnishings.

● Anchored to the walls for safety purposes, open shelves organize toys and games *left*. A cuckoo clock adorns the gabled top of the "barn."

● Ginghams, plaids, checks, dots, and stripes adorn the anything-goes kid's room *opposite*. The cartoonlike garden theme ignores adult decorating rules, putting a child's individual tastes first. The lavender picket fence and giant sunflowers are constructed of foam-core board, balsa wood, thick dowels, and foam-rubber leaves.

Blue Skies Ahead continued on page 69

Blue Skies Ahead continued from page 66

● Outdoor motifs of grass and sky *left* combine with garden-found treasures to bring the outside in. Cheerful color fills every inch of the space, from the wildly painted furnishings to the fanciful walls.

● The window seat *above*, made comfy with pillows and padding, is perfect for reading and relaxing. When not in use, it is a great place to stash stuffed toys.

ACTIVITY CENTER DESIGN

If you plan your child's room with each of his or her activities in mind, you may be able to reclaim control of other family gathering areas. Design each area of the child's room to accommodate a regular activity, such as studying, reading, drawing, playing, practicing an instrument, dribbling a ball, or perfecting a plié. Include ample, easy-to-reach storage in each defined area to increase the likelihood of occasional voluntary cleanup. Choose surfaces and accessories that are appropriate for the activity (for example, easy-to-clean flooring in the art center or hardwood floors for dribbling a ball). For more information on room arranging, see pages 126 and 127.

TUSCAN SUNSET. More peaceful than a primary scheme, the earthy palette of this European-inspired room evokes a sense of tranquillity. The ambience is calm and inviting rather than busy. To keep the palette from looking overly adult, youthful block-print fabrics adorn the bedding and valance.

The custom-made bed frame serves as an attractive focal point. Constructed from medium-density fiberboard, the faux-painted showpiece resembles worn wood and stone. The headboard frames a trompe l'oeil view of the Tuscan countryside.

Highly textured walls, awning valances, and distressed trim and shutters give the space an alfresco feel. A stone compound combined with several layers of glazes mixed with amber and wheat-color paints gives dimension to all of the painted surfaces. A faux tray ceiling carries the wall finish 1½ feet beyond the ceiling edge. A small molding helps encourage the illusion, but trompe l'oeil renderings complete the effect with artful ceiling angles in warmer, darker hues. Simple, old-fashioned awning valances invite the outdoors in. To give the window trim and shutters a weathered appearance, red and wheat-color paints were randomly blotted over a beige base coat; then blue paint was dragged over the top.

● Sunset colors and trompe l'oeil effects send the newly decorated space *left* back to another place and time. Antique toys add authenticity to the old-fashioned ambience.

● The walls *right* look centuries old, thanks to the application of a stone compound covered with several layers of glazes and paints. **For more decorative painting and glazing techniques, see pages 110–112.**

POLKA-DOT PERFECTION. One color is nice—but a rainbow is so much nicer. Everything in this room springs from the bold color combinations found in a ready-made spotted quilt. Affordable striped and solid sheets complement the cheerful spots without creating pattern overload.

Fanciful touches include a playful butterfly pillow sham, colorful rag dolls, and multiple round braided chenille rugs. The washable rugs bring in lively color, more round shapes, and inviting texture; they also protect the wood floor from everyday spills and other mishaps that are commonplace in a young child's room. Dotted window sheers, a round bedside table, and ball finials on the bed frame further emphasize the polka-dot theme.

Woven storage baskets underneath the bed fit into the vivid rainbow color scheme. The yellow bed was specially requested by the occupant; soft green eggshell-finish walls prevent the sunny primary tone from overpowering the room. The round side table was painted the same green as the walls to keep the focus on the beaded-board headboard and colorful accessories. A zigzag-shape wooden table skirt gives the simple table extra weight, making it look proportionate beside the sturdy twin-size bed.

● Dots and stripes are easy to mix and match. They provide lively color in this little girl's room *right*. The bed was custom-painted in a favorite color found in the ready-made quilt.

● Purchased unfinished, the round side table *left* was coated in the same color paint as the walls, but in a high-gloss finish. A colorful rag doll and painted photo frame reinforce the color scheme and personalize the room.

For furniture customizing ideas, see pages 15, 29, and 121–123.

●**VERSATILE BEDDING** If you plan to purchase ready-made bedding, you may want to use it as a starting point for your decorating scheme. Don't limit your selections to the children's department; this colorful quilt could easily serve an adult or a child.

teen retreats

teenretreats

Let your teen make the decorating decisions for his or her room, and there's a chance he or she may be proud enough of the space to occasionally pick it up.

STARRY NIGHTS. Hobbies, sports, and favorite interests are great starting points for the decor in a preteen's room. An 11-year-old's love of astronomy determined the design theme for this starry room. Here, a budding space explorer can view the real night sky through the minimally treated window—or pick out new constellations on the painted walls and ceiling. Adorned with hand-painted stars, galaxies, and a moon, the midnight blue backdrop evokes nearly the same sense of wonder as the actual night sky. The educational undercurrent is a bonus most parents appreciate; accessories such as a microscope, a telescope (not shown), and books are provided to make learning easy.

Bright yellow bedding provides invigorating contrast against the deep blue walls and keeps the room from looking too dark. The boxed-corner comforter simplifies daily bed-making. A valance made to match the comforter tops the window. Vibrant plaid throw pillows and a tailored bed skirt with big decorative buttons mix up the blue and yellow. Above the bed, a painted peg rack decked with a city skyline mimics a mountaintop or aerial view of a city at night.

● A twin bed *far right* leaves room for spreading out with friends. Tough berber carpeting makes floor cleanup easy.

● More than a place to hang a hat, the peg rack *right* enhances the sky and outer space theme by offering an aerial view of a city skyline.

For decorative painting instructions for these starry sky walls, see page 124.

PERSONAL EXPRESSION. Cheerful colors, playful accessories, and a mix of vintage and new fabrics transform a ho-hum room into a personality-packed space. The furnishings are tag sale or discount store finds. To give the mismatched pieces a visual connection, each was sanded, primed, and coated with a high-gloss white paint. For extra design punch, the headboard, footboard, and nightstand were accented with the same blue paint that was used on the walls. Funky yellow dots painted on the headboard and footboard tie together the paint and fabric selections. A painted polka-dot wall border carries the look throughout the room.

The throw at the end of the bed was made from a queen-size flannel sheet that was folded in half, sewn together, and stuffed with thick batting. The fringe trim gives the throw extra decorative flair. Peppy homespun pillows plump up the head of the bed. The phrase "rest your head" adorns the patchwork squares on the center blue pillow. The small, soft pillow is made from a child's old cardigan sweater. The pink and yellow sham was fashioned from a vintage bedspread, which was also used to make the curtain panels.

The white border that surrounds the grouping of photos hung behind the bed is painted on the wall. Two different wallpapers serve as matting for each black and white photo.

● Fabric flowers with ribbon stems form a valance over bright curtain panels *above left* that were made from a chenille bedspread.

● Flowing ribbons and stylized flowers sewn on the bedding and window treatments *above* combine with playfully painted furnishings to give this bedroom one-of-a-kind flair. A colorful braided rug warms the wood floor and makes the room look complete.

● Floral pillow shams and pillowcases with green, grasslike felt edgings *opposite* give the bed extra color and style.

For project instructions, see pages 120 and 121.

WHAT'S YOUR STYLE? The projects featured here can easily be adapted to match any taste. Switching the color scheme and replacing ribbons with natural twine could give the room a masculine flair. Omit the curvy scalloped edges and replace them with zigzags for a contemporary twist. Trade in the sweet sweater pillow for a favorite team jersey or flannel shirt version. Replace flowers with any motif close to your child's heart, such as softballs for a budding pitcher or guitars for a musician.

SILHOUETTES AND PILLOW FIGHTS. A mural depicting a slumber-party pillow fight—complete with real pillows and strategically glued feathers—is the focal point of this teen haven. The two teenage-girl images were first projected onto the wall, then their outlines were filled in with black paint. Pillowcases and feathers attached to the wall with hot glue were positioned to look as though they are in motion.

To keep attention on the mural, the furnishings and accessories are simple and straightforward: a side-by-side dresser and desk, a full-size bed topped with a white cotton comforter and rich chenille throw, and a red and white check bed skirt and neck roll pillow. Window treatments include gauzy curtains adorned with a tab-top valance in a botanical print.

● A tailored bed skirt, a soft chenille throw, and a nubby bedspread add enticing texture to the teen's room *left*. Hand-painted silhouettes add a sense of liveliness and motion.

● The pillowcase and feathers *below* are simply hot-glued to the wall, creating a funky three-dimensional effect that increases the illusion of motion.

SILHOUETTES AND 3-D TOUCHES

The images on this bedroom wall were created by drawing the girls' outlines freehand on transparencies, projecting them onto the wall with an overhead projector, and tracing around them with a pencil. If freehand drawing is not your talent, cut out the subjects from actual photos, tape them onto transparencies to project onto the wall, and trace the projected images using a black pencil. For either method, fill in the outlines with black latex or acrylic paint.

The mural in this room is successful because it shows movement: The combination of swirling feathers and rumpled pillowcases makes the mural appear three-dimensional. To give the pillows dimension, cut pillow shapes from foam-core board; then glue fiberfill to the foam-core pillow shapes. Next, glue pillowcases over the forms, wrapping and securing the fabric on the back to create the right fit. Use hot glue to attach the pillows and feathers to the wall. Paint curved lines around the feathers to increase the sense of motion.

INDUSTRIAL DIVIDE. Privacy is a big issue for teens, and a room divider is one way to offer them more of it, especially if two are sharing the space. The divider in this bedroom, made from inexpensive home center materials, separates a sitting area from a more private sleeping area behind it. Crafted from 2×4s, sheet metal, and roofing plastic, the industrial divider sets the contemporary tone for the rest of the room. Bold colors add warmth and chenille bedspreads and antique iron bed frames provide textural contrast to the metal partition.

A 5-inch-deep galvanized metal channel runs the length of an adjacent wall in the sitting area, offering display space for a colorful collection of lava lamps. Bold wire mesh chairs stand out against the inlay of inexpensive black automobile carpeting. Sheet metal wrapped around two plywood disks and topped with lava rocks serves as a coffee table. Behind the table, the metal panels are a forum for magnetic words. A combination of file cabinets and vintage metal school lockers provides all the necessary storage.

Overhead light fixtures, made from conduit and shop lights, brighten both sides of the room. Giant graphic drawings of utensils and tools hang in pairs, like a couple of siblings.

● Light flows through the plastic panels of the partition *below*. One side of the partition features smooth sheet metal; the other side has corrugated metal panels.

● Jewel-tone bedding in solid green, red, amethyst, and yellow *opposite top* complements the vibrant walls and allows each occupant to express individuality with personal color selections.

● A black painted wooden bench *opposite bottom* offers seating near the beds. Hard-wearing cream-color berber carpet adds texture and light to the room.

SHARED SUCCESS

Sharing a room with a sibling can teach lessons that last a lifetime, including compromise, cooperation, negotiation, and respect for others' possessions. Sharing works best if roommates are the same sex and close in age. Putting a toddler with a preteen or teenager can create problems for both. Sleep schedules and privacy needs are very different, and your older child may find it difficult to keep his or her portion of the room babyproof. To foster sharing while meeting the needs of each individual, keep these design guidelines in mind:

Make color compromises. Let each child select colors, patterns, and bed linens from an agreed-upon color palette such as brights or pastels. Signature colors can help identify personal spaces and possessions.

Carve out personal space. All children need some space of their own. Whether it's room for art or science projects or shelves for sports collectibles, provide teens with enough space so they can pursue individual interests and goals.

Minimize clutter with multipurpose furniture. Add storage headboards, an armoire that stores more than a computer, and rolling bins under the beds.

EMPHASIZING ART

In this bedroom, the horizontal placement of art doubles as a headboard, making the wall complete. The prints would not have the same impact if they were scattered on the walls throughout the room. The white frames connect the art to the white woodwork and bedding.

If you have a large expanse of wall to decorate, look for complementary pictures or photos and display them in similar frames to appear as one large piece of art. For a contemporary look, hang the pieces to form a perfect square or rectangle, as shown.

COOL AND SOPHISTICATED. Green and blue stripes combine with framed prints and minimal furnishings to create a room that is both lively and serene, a combination of attitudes fitting for a teen's retreat. The four colorfully matted photos, set against vivid striped walls, double as an inexpensive headboard. Oversize mats and glossy white frames give the 4×6 snapshots more attention.

Black and white pillows, a black and white stripe bed skirt, and a white down comforter invite relaxation while keeping the focus on the walls. Contemporary side tables, bedside lamps, and a folding chair complete the sleek look.

● Wide stripes in cool tones walk the line between subtle and daring in the sophisticated teen bedroom *opposite*. The cool tones are smooth, but they're saturated enough to pack a colorful punch.

● Allow your teen to take pictures of a subject he or she is interested in, such as architecture, nature, or sports; then frame the prints using colorful oversize mats. The photos shown *above* are 4×6 snapshots framed in 16×20-inch mats and fit into inexpensive white frames.

For information on how to paint striped walls, see page 25.

BLUE HUES. A favorite color—blue—served as the starting point for this teen's room. To prevent color overload, the shade and texture of each surface was purposely varied.

Collected from yard sales and flea markets, a handful of vintage 1970s pieces add retro charm to the room: a credenza turned dresser, an armchair, a bench, and a globe. A pair of midcentury Eames chairs, which regained popularity in the '70s, flank the fireplace.

Two broad, shiny blue stripes encompass the bottom half of the room; a swatch of white chenille fabric separates them. A pale shade of blue softens the walls above the stripes. On the floor, rectangles of hook-and-loop blue carpets are bound together to soften the dark hardwood floor. Suedelike fabric adorned with windowpane checks covers the twin beds; a navy throw and fluffy white faux-fur pillows break up the large expanses of color. Framed prints, matte chrome beds, miniblinds, and groovy glass vases complete the youthful looking space.

● Big stretches of blue throughout the room *left* create the cool ambience the occupant of this space desired. No longer in service, the old fireplace now serves as a spot for storing sports equipment.

● The 1970s retro look, extremely popular in teen clothing lines, is making its way into room decor by way of vintage furnishings and accessories as shown *below*. The faux-fur pillows are inexpensive discount store finds that suit and soften the overall look.

LAVENDER AND LACE. A teen girl's favorite fabric inspired the design theme of this feminine room: The sheer curtain panels feature an appliquéd flower-and-vine design, which was the starting point for a stencil motif that would soon spread to the walls, bed linens, and window seat cushion. All of these surfaces are a perfect canvas for stenciled designs.

The lacy floral design from the window sheers was enlarged and stenciled in white over tranquil lavender walls and decorative pillows; the color scheme was reversed on the bed linens and seat cushion. For continuity, the stencils on the linens were created using the same lavender paint that was used on the walls.

A painted wooden cornice completes the window treatment without detracting from the stenciled design or lace panels. Tailored piping adds a polished decorative detail to the lavender

pillows, which are wrapped in the sheer curtain fabric Next to the window seat, a feather boa-style floor lamp teams with the white accent pillows to soften the look even further.

● The serene color scheme *right* is soft and delicate, creating an inviting ambience for the resident teenage girl.

● White linens *left* provide a crisp counterpoint to the lavender walls while offering a perfect canvas for the stenciled design.

For more information on stenciling walls and fabrics, see pages 116 and 117.

●DO IT YOURSELF Purchase ready-made stencils at a crafts or art supply store. If you can't find a ready-made stencil that matches your decor, consider making your own. Fabric, wrapping paper, greeting cards, framed artwork, dishware, and books contain design inspiration, but take care to comply with all copyright laws before duplicating any designs. Trace the desired designs onto clear acetate sheets—available at crafts and art supply stores—and cut them out with a sharp crafts or utility knife. Use a ruler to make straight cuts.

specialspaces

specialspaces

Playrooms, gathering spaces, and baths welcome children when you include some of these clever, easy-to-achieve design ideas.

CREATIVE PLAY. Climbing stairs may tax tired grown-ups, but for kids with limitless energy, bounding up the stairs is no sweat, particularly when something fun awaits at the top. Once nothing more than a broad hallway at the top of the kitchen stairs, this area is now a kid magnet. The madeover space keeps clutter out of the public parts of the house and puts kids a mere holler away from Mom or Dad. And because the children's bedrooms are nearby, toys can move from room to room without cluttering other spaces.

Paint transforms the previously white hallway ceiling into a cloud-filled sky adorned with the famous Peter Pan quote "You can fly." An artist painted this design, but stencils can help you achieve a similar look.

The oak plank floor features a painted winding track for toy cars and trucks and game boards for hopscotch and checkers. A geometric pattern in bold colors brings the walls to life. Books, toys, and a TV and VCR stow in a custom-made entertainment center.

● Located in a wide hallway adjacent to the children's bedrooms, the play area *right* gives kids fun floor space, away from busier areas where they might be underfoot.

For instructions on how to paint a racetrack on a wood floor, see page 118. For advice on how to find a mural painter, see page 35. For additional mural painting advice, see page 45.

SPACE-SAVING IDEAS

If space is limited, design a dual-functioning room. For example, a guest bedroom with a daybed trundle leaves enough floor space for a toddler table or toy car track. When you aren't entertaining overnight guests, the bed can hold stuffed toys and serve as a place for kids to relax and read.

A basement can easily double as a play area and a family gathering space if you define clear boundaries. Fill one end of the room with child-size furnishings, toys, and storage shelves and the other with comfy upholstered pieces and audiovisual equipment.

● PLAY SPACE BASICS Anything goes when you're choosing patterns and colors for a play space. To give children a sense of pride and accomplishment, let them help with the palette selection for the walls, ceiling, and even the woodwork.

To make playroom cleanup manageable, choose scrubbable paint finishes and cover upholstered pieces with washable slipcovers in busy patterns to

HIDE AND SEEK. Bold color and private hideaways entice children to come, play, and stay for a while. Each wall in this second-floor play space is painted a different color, serving as a backdrop for an array of toys and games including beanbag chairs shaped like sports balls.

● Under-the-eaves space *left* serves as a hideout. Bookshelves set on hinges act as a secret door that leads to a hidden passageway. The walls inside the hideout are coated with chalkboard paint so children can leave secret messages and draw treasure-hunt maps.

● On another wall of the playroom, an antique ladder provides access to a loft *below*. Vibrantly painted balusters provide a safety wall without limiting the view, so children in the loft still feel like part of the action in the main room.

elp disguise drips and spills. Install open helves low on the wall and add plenty of storage ins so children can pitch in and help pick up.

Put an easel in the playroom to encourage udding artists. Protect the floor below it with an nexpensive floorcloth. To protect your child's lothing, keep old shirts or smocks on hand.

KID CONNECTION. The upstairs in this house is reserved for children—and the fire pole in the playroom is the main attraction. The pole is identical to those used in many firehouses and connects the second-level playroom to the first-floor family room. A safety lid prevents falls and buffers noise between the playroom and gathering area below.

The built-in desk is topped with open shelves that store toys, books, and audio equipment. A wood plank floor easily withstands daily use and sweeps clean in minutes. A built-in bench below the window holds toys and dolls.

Vivid periwinkle walls provide a cheery background for white woodwork and built-ins. Framed custom artwork, painted by the youngest residents, adorns the walls. A combination of downlights and wall sconces keeps the area bright and cheerful, day and night.

● Open and bright, the spare room *right* serves as a perfect zone for fun. Messes aren't a problem because the room is upstairs, out of sight from the main-floor gathering areas.

● The fire pole provides a fast slide from the play area to the family room, making this house a popular gathering place for neighborhood children. A safety lid *below* is a must for home-installed poles. Lids such as this should always be secured by an adult.

POLE POINTS

If you are thinking of installing a fire pole in your home, check local building codes to see if your community has restrictions against them. If you can legally install a pole, visit a local firehouse first to look at the construction and to decide whether you and your children will be comfortable with it.

This pole features a custom two-part lid with an overlapping safety lip. Cover the opening when young children are present. A periodic application of brass cleaner ensures a smooth ride. To maintain family peace, set rules against throwing things down the hatch or pressuring anyone who doesn't want to slide. For fun, keep a "pole book" similar to a guest registry for first-time riders to sign.

HOMEWORK HAVENS. Word processing and poster board projects are common homework assignments. Planning a special space to accommodate them saves your child time—and you the headache of moving everything on and off the kitchen island or dining room table.

The family room featured here makes space for both homework and leisure activities. On one side, the kids can play air hockey or watch movies on a big-screen TV. On the other side, a built-in study area features three workstations with computers, drawers, and cabinets for reference books and supplies. A central built-in entertainment unit divides the spaces so the TV cannot be seen from the homework area.

● Chalkboard panels, obtained from a school supply company, and durable

beaded board painted gray *opposite* run the perimeter of the room. A similar look can be achieved with affordable, easy-to-use chalkboard paint, as explained *below*.

● The 4×8-foot chalkboard panels *opposite below* are nailed into the drywall and trimmed with molding.

● At the desk *left*, corkboard spray-painted black provides a perfect spot to post memos and reminders.

● To conserve space, the computer monitors *below* are secured to the wall with monitor screen mounts purchased from a medical supply store.

INSTANT CHALKBOARD

Create an instant doodle space on bedroom, bath, or playroom walls (or doors or furnishings) with chalkboard paint, available at home centers and crafts stores. One coat covers most surfaces and dries overnight. Manufacturers offer a variety of color choices to coordinate with decors.

CLUTTER BUSTERS. As any parent knows, with kids comes clutter. Organizing it helps keep the house manageable and reduces the daily stress associated with getting everyone out the door on time.

The family entryway is typically the most difficult area to keep clean and clutter-free. To help manage shoes, backpacks, and an endless array of sports equipment and toys, consider installing one locker for each child. On an opposite or adjacent wall, install a bulletin board to catch soccer schedules, party invitations, messages, and other household paperwork that ordinarily piles up on a desk or countertop. Add a file cabinet or mailboxes labeled with each child's name to store school papers. If you live in an area where it snows or rains a lot, consider installing a floor drain near the back door where family members can deposit wet shoes and boots.

To give children a creative outlet in the kitchen, replace a plain dishwasher panel with a chalkboard; then set a pretty cup filled with colorful chalks on the counter nearby. The chalkboard can also double as a family

message center. A dry-erase white board installed behind doors in the family room lets kids play games and doodle without creating clutter on the floor or tables. A back-door bulletin board also serves as a display space for artwork.

● Located near the garage and deck doors, the wall of lockers *opposite left* is convenient for children of any height.

● Pretty coat hooks installed between framed family pictures transform a back hallway *opposite top* into a coatroom. The photos serve as labels for each family member's hook. The wicker drawer cabinet is on casters, so it can roll conveniently onto the scene or out of the way.

● Wasted space becomes play space when a customized chalkboard replaces the original front panel of a dishwasher *opposite bottom right*.

● A wall organizer *left* curtails paper clutter.

● The built-in bench *below left* provides a spot to take off and put on footwear. Hooks let kids put coats away with a quick toss.

● A dry-erase board, concealed behind family room cabinetry *below right*, gives children a harmless way to draw on the wall. It's also a practical spot for parents to help with spelling lessons or math equations.

BATH BASICS. Creating a bath to meet the functional and aesthetic needs of two or more children is a difficult assignment—and a common one. Privacy is essential. In a standard 5×8-foot bath, for example, consider installing a shoji screen, a partial wall, or a full wall and a doorway to separate the vanity from the toilet and tub. This way, two children can use different areas of the bath at the same time and still maintain privacy. Installing double sinks, or even a single sink with a long expanse of counter, allows two children to groom side by side without

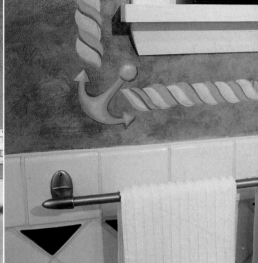

bumping elbows.

Take some of the pressure off a shared space by adding a grooming center to each child's bedroom. For example, top a stand-alone desk or low dresser with a mirror; place it near accessible electric outlets (providing your children are old enough to operate electrical appliances), so that hair dryers and curling irons can be plugged in.

No space to spare? If these space-sharing strategies are outside the realm of possibility, work out a schedule in which each sibling gets his or her turn in the bath for a specified time that fits within activity and sleep schedules.

● In the 6×13-foot bath *opposite,* a wall and a hinged door separate the toilet and tub from the vanity. At each end of the vanity, a recessed medicine cabinet expands storage space.

● Opposite the vanity mirror, a niche recessed only 4 inches into the stud wall *above left* provides display space.

● A cobalt blue colorwash applied over light blue paint on the wall *above right* creates a watery, sealike ambience. Hand-painted anchor and rope embellishments complete the nautical theme.

● Pegs attached to the back of the door *left* make it easy for children to hang up towels.

For wall painting techniques, see pages 110–112.

PICTURE-BOOK PRETTY. Young at heart but far from childish, this bath was designed to take a 10-year-old through her teen years. White floor and wall tiles and white cabinetry and fixtures ensure a lasting foundation; if the girl's tastes evolve, the painted walls, shower curtains, and window treatments can be updated in an afternoon.

Where the wall tile ends, an enchanting wall mural begins. The pastoral masterpiece wraps around three of the walls, depicting a fanciful storybook landscape that includes a thatch-roof cottage, a tranquil pond, soaring birds, and the girl's favorite: fluttering butterflies. The custom-painted mural reflects her preference for yellows, pinks, and outdoor play.

At the window, a lush gathered valance of textured yellow cotton hangs atop a balloon shade of white handkerchief eyelet, creating a petticoat effect. The same fabrics appear in the curtain panels that frame the shower enclosure, softening

the hard tile surround and the overall look of the room.

A two-tiered countertop provides a makeup vanity for the girl to play at now and to primp at later. Glass shelves above the toilet offer pretty storage and display space.

● The pastoral theme of the wall mural *left* charms children and adult guests who visit this little girl's bath. The mural transforms a once uninviting corridor into an artistic focal point.

● A creative blend of ceramic tiles adds texture and dimension to the walls surrounding a makeup counter *above*. The area was remodeled to meet the needs of a 10-year-old as she matures into a teen.

● Shapely border tiles frame the mirror above the sink *right* and create an attractive crown molding. The slip-resistant floor tiles promote safety and complement the marble countertop.

For wall mural painting advice, see pages 35 and 45.

BATH PLANNING. Whatever the ages and abilities of your children, design your bath to make each user as independent, comfortable, and safe as possible. Even if no one in your home has special needs now, including a bath that can accommodate people of all abilities will make guests—and even a kid with a cast—feel more comfortable.

● The charming barrier-free bath *below* provides drive-in grooming space for a sports car enthusiast, including enough clear floor space for a complete wheelchair turnaround. The tile floors have the right amount of grip for wheelchair maneuvering, and the sink is equipped with a hydraulically operated system, complete with anti-scald faucets that can be raised or lowered at the touch of a switch.

● Blocks of color bring childlike energy to the predominantly white bath *opposite top left*. Planned for a sister and brother, the compact bath maximizes storage and counter space to dispel territorial bickering.

Because the siblings aren't yet tall enough to use the mirrors on the wall-mounted cabinets, a hinged center mirror meets current grooming needs. The adjustable feature will serve the pair as they grow, accommodating a height difference between them, should that become an issue.

● The confettilike tiles that line the shower *opposite top right* also cover the lower half of the walls throughout the room; a fun paper-doll wallpaper covers the upper half. Complementary slip-resistant floor tile combine safety with durability—the tiled surfaces can stand up to even the wettest of water fights. Towels stacked in the linen closet are easily reachable for a child of any height.

● Floorcloths like the one shown *opposite bottom* are an inexpensive way to add safe nonskid floor coverings to a child's bath. **For instructions on how to create a floorcloth, see page 125.**

NUMBERS TO KNOW

Plan for a door opening of 34 inches. Larger doors are hard to open and close from a seated position, and narrower openings make it difficult, if not impossible, for a wheelchair to get through.

For a typical-size wheelchair to make a complete turnaround, you'll need to leave an area of clear floor space measuring 5 feet in diameter. Leave a 30×48-inch area in front of the sink. Clear floor space can overlap in front of the tub. Leave 60 inches square in front of the tub. Toilets need a clear floor space that is 48 inches square.

Shower stalls are easier to get in and out of than tubs. Choose a stall with little or no threshold. The stall should measure at least 4 feet square, with an opening 36 inches wide. Include a built-in bench that is 17 to 19 inches tall, a single-handle water control lever, a handheld shower spray, and grab bars.

Provide knee space under the sink about 27 inches high and 30 inches wide. Insulate or conceal hot-water pipes to protect users from scalding.

A toilet 3 inches taller than a conventional model makes it easier to transfer to and from a wheelchair. Install grab bars 33 to 36 inches above the floor on all the sidewalls by the toilet.

●**BATHROOM SAFETY** Incorporate these tips in your bath design to help protect your child:

Install grab bars throughout to provide stability for all users, whatever their age.

Choose slip-resistant flooring, such as textured floor tiles or sheet vinyls.

Select rugs with nonskid backings or create themed floorcloths.

Install rubber feet on all step stools and chairs to prevent them from slipping when in use.

Round off countertop and cabinetry corners and pad all other sharp corners with foam rubber.

Keep medicines and cleaning supplies in childproof cabinets. Flush old medicines down the toilet.

To prevent possible electrocution, ensure that all electrical outlets are equipped with ground fault circuit interrupters. Place outlets so kids can't reach plugged-in appliances; outlets behind locked cabinet doors are ideal.

To prevent scalding, reduce hot-water temperature to 120 degrees Fahrenheit or install easy-to-operate anti-scald faucets. Available at home centers and plumbing supply stores, these faucets regulate water temperature when there is a change in pressure due to another appliance or fixture being turned on or off.

To help prevent cuts and bruises, add a waterproof cushion to the tub spout. Cushions in various shapes are available at many bath and hardware centers.

decoratingideas

childstyle ideas&projects

A

Add a personal touch to your child's room with a few of the simple decorating projects in this chapter. Work with your child to plan a one-of-a-kind glaze treatment for the walls, or surprise him or her with new wallpaper and a "made by Mom and Dad" window treatment. Projects include a brightly painted floorcloth, custom painted furniture, and a pillow made from a too-small sweater. Also included are room arrangement strategies for children of all ages.

DECORATIVE GLAZING TECHNIQUES

The mottled look that adds depth to decoratively painted walls and other surfaces comes courtesy of glaze. Affordably priced, standard glaze dries clear and makes paint translucent, allowing you to create thin layers of colors for a mottled effect. Water-base glazes are ideal for do-it-yourselfers: Paint is typically stirred into the glaze to create the perfect color for your painting project. The more or less paint you add, the darker or lighter the effect. Some stores sell tinted glazes that are ready to apply to walls, with no mixing required. Look for glazing products at home centers and at paint, art supply, and crafts stores.

Experiment First

Before you put a brush to the wall, practice glazing techniques on a primed piece of foam-core board. Experiment with the following basic techniques for applying glazes:

■ **Positive application.** In a positive application, you add a glaze/paint mixture to a surface: Dip a glazing tool into the colored glaze, wring out or dab off the excess glaze, and lightly apply the glaze to the wall. Always use a flat or eggshell base coat that is a shade or two lighter than the glaze. Positive applications add a visible yet subtle texture to a wall.

■ **Negative application.** In a negative application, you remove glaze painted onto a base-coated surface: Remove some of the glaze by rolling or dabbing it away, revealing the base coat while adding texture and pattern. Always use a semigloss or satin base coat. Negative applications typically yield stronger patterns than positive applications do.

Tips for Successful Painting

■ **To ensure a consistent look** throughout a room, use closely related base and glaze colors, such as light blue and medium blue. Stark contrasts can be hard to blend and to repeat. When you are satisfied with the paint-to-glaze ratio, record it for future reference, but mix enough glaze to do all the walls, because another batch may not yield an exact match.

■ **Work in 2- to 3-foot sections** so the glaze does not dry before you are done. Apply tools lightly to the wall surface. In positive applications, heavy pressure can leave too much glaze on the wall, blurring the pattern.

■ **To avoid double layers** of glaze in the corners,

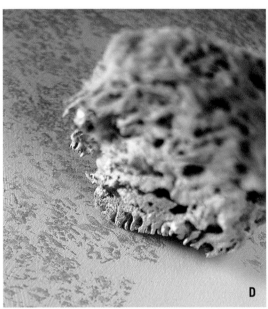

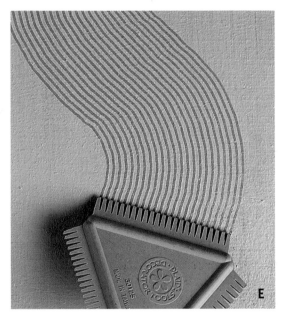

tape off the adjacent walls, apply the glaze, and let it dry. Then tape the glazed wall and work on glazing the adjacent wall.

■ **If you make a mistake,** brush over the area with the base coat, let dry, and reglaze the section.

Glazing Tools and Effects

A. Cheesecloth: If you're looking for a subtle texture, use cheesecloth. Dab the cloth in glaze, blot off the excess, and scrunch the cloth onto the wall. Or apply glaze with a roller and then remove it using a light dabbing motion.

B. Paintbrush: A basic paintbrush can produce a stunning stripe finish, called strié. Roll a light-color glaze onto the walls. Then brush over the glaze, wiping off the paintbrush with a clean dry rag after each swipe. To create a woven clothlike

pattern, brush over the glaze in an X pattern.

C. Texture-giving tools: Mopping tools and mitts are alternatives to cheesecloth and sponges, but you use them in the same way. Dip a tool in glaze and blot; then pounce it onto a wall. Or roll glaze onto the wall and then remove it with the tool, wiping the tool with a clean dry rag after each section.

D. Sea sponge: Sponges create soft-edge effects. First, dampen and soften a sea sponge with water. Use a light hand to add subtle layers of glaze to a lighter-color background, blotting and rotating the sponge often.

E. Comb: Use a comb to create straight or curvy lines or woven looks. First roll glaze onto the walls. Drag the comb through the glaze to create the desired pattern. Combine vertical and

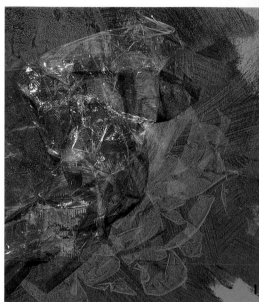

horizontal lines to create a burlap look.

F. Rag: Use a rolled-up rag to add loose pattern to walls. To get the look shown, roll walls with a lighter-color glaze. Twist the rag and dab it onto the wall to remove glaze. Rotate the rag for a varied pattern.

G. Stippling brush: Create textural dots all over your walls with a stippling brush. Roll a glaze that is slightly darker than the base coat onto the walls. Working quickly, pounce the brush in a tight pattern over the glaze. If necessary, wipe the brush to remove any excess glaze that builds up on it.

H. Crumpled paper: Crumple up plain brown bags, butcher paper, or blank newsprint. Lightly dip the paper into the glaze and dab off the excess. Pounce the glaze-covered paper onto the wall to

create this crinkled look.

I. Plastic wrap: Bunch up plastic wrap or sandwich bags; then lightly dip the plastic into the glaze and dab off the excess. Pounce the glaze-covered plastic onto the walls to create markings that resemble plaster. A similar look can be achieved with a negative application: Apply glaze to the wall with a paintbrush. Then spread sheets of plastic onto the wall and peel them off.

WALLPAPERING SUPPLIES

Gather all tools and supplies before starting any wallpapering project. The following tools are available from paint and wallcovering retailers and from most home centers:

- Wallpaper stripper
- Wallpaper
- Wallpaper primer
- Carpenter's level
- Water tray
- Wallpaper brush
- Plumb bob
- Seam roller
- Razor knife with several extra blades or razor knife with break-off blades
- Straightedge
- Scraper
- Scissors
- Damp cloth/sponge
- Screwdrivers
- Drop cloths

WALLPAPERING BASICS

If you prefer wallpapering over painting, you are in luck: Wallpapers are easier to hang than they used to be. With planning and patience, you can wallpaper a bedroom in a weekend. Before choosing a paper, consider your experience level, the features of the room, and the look you desire. Some patterns, like stripes, are easier for novices to hang because there is no pattern to match; however, it can be difficult to keep stripes straight on crooked walls and stripes can accentuate flaws in the wall surface. Other papers, such as florals and busy patterns, require matching, but the busyness of the design often distracts from imperfections in the walls or the hanging.

Calculating Rolls

To estimate the number of rolls of wallcovering you'll need, measure the square footage around the room by multiplying wall height by total wall width. Divide the result by the square footage of one single roll of your chosen wallcovering (coverage amounts differ depending upon paper selection). Wallcoverings are calculated in single rolls, but are often sold in double rolls (also called bolts), so you'll need to divide the result by 2. Always round up; do not deduct for openings such as doors, windows, or built-in shelving. This will allow for pattern matching, trimming, and waste.

Here is an example: If your room has 8-foot-high ceilings and four 10-foot-wide walls and your wallpaper has a coverage of 27 square feet per single roll, multiply 8 by 40, arriving at 320 square feet. Next, divide 320 square feet by 27 square feet to come up with 11.85 rolls. Round up this total to the nearest whole number: 12. Divide 12 by 2 to determine you'll need 6 double rolls to cover the room.

Consider ordering extra rolls for mistakes or later repairs, and keep a record of the pattern name or number and dye-lot number in case you have to reorder. Always ask a store associate to double-check roll calculations before ordering.

LINERS

Wallpaper liners make rough surfaces smooth enough for wallpapering. Essentially unprinted wallpaper stock, liners come in grades from lightweight (to help delicate wallcoverings, fabric wallcoverings, or grass cloths adhere) to heavy-duty (to provide a smooth surface over paneling, textured walls, tile, and cement block). Lining can also be used to stabilize old walls or to bridge hairline cracks.

1. Strip the old paper. It is best to remove existing wallpaper before applying new paper. Before beginning, protect baseboards and floors with drop cloths to catch stripper drips and wallpaper scraps. If removal isn't possible, old wallpaper that is firmly attached can be left in place and covered with a new layer. Cover the old paper with wallpaper primer—see Step 2— to hide the pattern and to provide a good bonding surface. Do not match up the new seams with the old ones.

To remove old paper, work a corner of the wallcovering loose and pull it carefully. If the wallcovering pulls away some of the wall surface, use wallpaper stripper in liquid or gel form to loosen the paper. Note that gels tend to be less messy than liquids and soak into the paper

better. Remove the paper with a scraper. If the wallpaper doesn't loosen, the stripper hasn't penetrated the surface. Score the wallpaper carefully with a wallpaper-scraping tool. Reapply the stripper and continue scraping until all the paper is removed. Using a damp cloth or sponge, clean any remaining residue off the wall and let the surface dry.

2. Prepare the walls. Fix wall damage, such as cracks, flaking paint, and holes. To ensure a strong bond, clean the wall and cover it with a primer designed for wallcovering applications. To help conceal any small gaps in seams, have the primer custom tinted to match the wallcovering background. Wallpaper primers eliminate the need for sizing. The primer seals the wall, helps the wallpaper bond better, and creates a surface with good "slide," making wallpaper easier to manipulate for pattern matching. In addition, a wallpaper primer also makes wallcoverings easier to remove when you're ready for a change.

3. Mark plumb lines. Choose an inconspicuous corner—often behind a door, where pattern mismatching will be least obvious—for a starting point. Use a plumb bob to mark a straight, vertical line on the wall: Tack the string to the wall 2 inches from the top; let the bob hang 2 inches from the floor. When the bob stops swinging, hold the string taut against the wall and snap the string so it leaves a light chalk mark. This line indicates a true vertical. Establish another true vertical line when you turn a corner or start a new section of wall.

4. Prepare the covering. Cut the first strip of wallcovering 6 inches longer than the section of the wall you're covering; it will overlap 3 inches at the top and bottom for trimming. For prepasted papers, roll the strip print side up and immerse it in a tray filled with water. Let the covering soak for the amount of time specified in the manufacturer's directions. Unroll the paper as you remove it from the tray, and lay the strip on a clean, washable surface, paste side up. If you are using paper that isn't prepasted, apply paste to the dry wallpaper (do not soak in water).

"Book" the strip by loosely folding—but not creasing—both ends so they meet in the middle; this keeps the paste from touching the front of the paper. Let the strip sit for the time indicated by the manufacturer so the paste can activate and the paper can expand and contract.

5. Apply the covering. Hang the first strip by unfolding the top end (leave the bottom end folded for the time being), holding it up by the corners, and lining it up with the plumb line. Allow 3 inches of wallcovering to overhang at the top edge for trimming. Unfold the bottom half of the strip and continue to align the strip with the plumb line. Allow the bottom 3 inches of the strip to overhang.

6. Smooth out bubbles. Using a soft brush and sweeping movements, smooth out wrinkles and air pockets. Use this technique for each strip as you hang it: Start at the top middle of each strip and work the brush diagonally to the right. Go back to the top middle and brush to the left so your motions form a triangle. Sponge off any wet paste that seeps to the front of the paper.

7. Align the next strips. Continue applying successive strips, aligning and smoothing the covering as described in Steps 5 and 6.

8. Trim off the excess. Trim excess wallcovering from top and bottom edges using a straightedge and sharp razor knife (a dull knife will tear the paper). Change the blade frequently to avoid tearing. Trim each strip while the paste is still damp; then flatten the seams gently but firmly using a seam roller. (Do not use seam rollers on embossed wallcoverings.) Sponge off any wet paste that seeps to the front of the paper.

9. Paper around doors and windows. Cut a rough opening in the dry strip that covers the door or window. Rough-cut the opening so that there are 3 extra inches of paper on all sides. Moisten the strip and hang it. Make diagonal cuts near the corners of the opening. Smooth the paper around the frame; trim and clean with a damp sponge.

10. Wallpaper around outlets and switchplates. Turn off electricity to the outlets and switches. Remove the electric outlet covers and switchplate covers before hanging the wallcovering. Position the wallcovering over the outlet or switch as though it isn't there, then cut an X with a razor knife over the outlet or switch opening. Smooth the paper into place. Trim the four flaps made by the X. Reattach the covers and turn the electricity back on.

11. Apply borders. Before applying borders over wallcoverings, let the wallcovering dry for 48 hours. To position borders, pencil a mark where the border will hang; use a level for perfect placement. Use vinyl-to-vinyl adhesive to hang the border, even if the border is prepasted. Borders need the extra adhesive to bond to a wallpaper's slicker surface.

For easier handling, fold a wet border accordion-style (without creasing), always keeping the adhesive side from touching the front. Have a helper hold each folded section as you prepare to apply it.

STENCILED FLOWER BORDER
SKILL LEVEL
Novice painter
SUPPLIES
- Stencils (purchased or homemade)
- Latex or acrylic paints or stenciling creams
- Stenciling brushes
- Paper plate
- Chalk and carpenter's level
- Low-tack painter's tape or spray adhesive

STENCILED FLOWER BED LINENS
SKILL LEVEL
Novice painter
SUPPLIES
- Stencils
- Textile medium
- Acrylic paint
- Paper plate
- Protective cover for work surface
- White cotton blend bed linens
- Stenciling brushes
- Low-tack painter's tape or spray adhesive

STENCILED FLOWER BORDER
(PROJECT SHOWN ON PAGE 89)

Whether you have the confidence of a master artist or first-timer jitters, you can stencil beautiful walls, fabrics, and furnishings. Here's what you need to know to get started:

- **To create a simple wall border** like the one shown *above,* position the stencil just below the ceiling line. Use low-tack tape or spray adhesive to keep the stencil in position.
- **Dip a stenciling brush** into the latex or acrylic paint (or stenciling cream). Dab the excess onto a paper plate. With a dabbing motion, stipple paint from the loaded brush into the design cutouts.
- **Line up the registration pattern** on the edge of the stencil and mark it with chalk. Using a carpenter's level to ensure a straight line, continue stenciling across the wall.

STENCILED FLOWER BED LINENS
(PROJECT SHOWN ON PAGE 88)

To ensure adequate coverage and to determine whether bleeding will be a problem, test a sample piece of fabric by applying acrylic paint mixed with textile medium to a laundered scrap or inconspicuous corner. Sturdy washable cotton-blend fabrics are the best choice.

- **Prior to stenciling,** launder the fabric, but don't use a fabric softener (it may prevent the paint from adhering to the fabric).
- **To further improve the bond** between the paint and the fabric fibers, mix textile medium (available at crafts stores) into the acrylic paint.
- **Lay the fabric on a protected work surface.** If you are stenciling pillowcases or other layered fabrics, line them with plastic bags, tucking the plastic tightly into the corners so paint won't soak through to the back.
- **Pull the fabric taut** and secure it to the work surface with tape. Tape the stencil in place on the fabric.
- **Dip a stenciling brush** into the paint and dab the excess onto a paper plate. With a dabbing motion, stipple paint from the loaded brush into the design cutouts.
- **Continue stenciling the fabric** in a random pattern, letting the paint dry before moving the stencil to a new location. When you are finished, let the fabric dry thoroughly.
- **To set the paint,** follow the textile medium manufacturer's directions (such as drying the fabric in a clothes dryer).

STENCILED FLOWER TEMPLATE

TIPS FOR FOOLPROOF STENCILING

▪ **Ready-made stencils** are available in a variety of motifs at crafts and art supply stores. Or create one-of-a-kind stencils by transferring designs to clear acetate sheets and cutting them out with a sharp crafts or utility knife, as shown *top right.*

▪ **Before starting a stenciling project,** experiment with paints. Thick stenciling creams won't seep under a stencil; acrylic paints are affordable, dry quickly, and offer an array of colors.

▪ **The short bristles on stenciling brushes,** shown *bottom right,* will do the best job of filling in intricate designs. Buy an assortment of sizes: Large brushes help fill in designs quickly; smaller brushes are best for detail work. Use one brush for each color to make the project progress as quickly and easily as possible. If you apply stencils in one color, use a small foam roller.

▪ **Use a chalk line** or a carpenter's level and chalk to mark vertical or horizontal lines for aligning stencils in a repeated pattern. The registration pattern (a portion of the stenciled design) at the left edge of the stencil makes aligning a repeated design easier. Use low-tack tape or spray adhesive to secure your stencil to the wall, furniture piece, or fabric. Adhesives prevent paint from seeping beneath the stencil, so the stenciled design has clean, crisp edges.

FLOOR PAINTING FUN
SKILL LEVEL
Experienced painter
SUPPLIES
- Sandpaper
- Chalk
- Paintbrushes: 3-inch flat and 1½-inch tapered; #10 flat artist's brush
- Latex floor paints in various colors
- White acrylic paint
- Black permanent marking pen
- Varnish or acrylic top coat

CUSTOM-COVERED LAMPSHADE
SKILL LEVEL
Novice crafter
SUPPLIES
- Plain fabric shade
- Decoupage paper or fabric
- Scissors
- Braid, ribbon, or beaded fringe
- Ready-made adornments for base
- Hot-glue gun and glue sticks

FLOOR PAINTING FUN
(PROJECT SHOWN ON PAGE 93)

Painted game boards and racetracks transform plain floors into enticing play areas. If your wood floor is in perfect condition, you may want to hire a professional to sand off the protective top coat and reapply it after you paint the desired motifs. If your wood floor is less than prime, add racetracks, game boards, and other adornments by following these simple instructions:

- **Sand off the top coating** and thoroughly clean the area you want to paint so that the floor paint will adhere well to the wood surface.
- **Referring to the photograph above,** chalk the design you want to paint onto the sanded floor.
- **Using the #10 flat brush** for corners and the 1½-inch tapered brush for interiors, paint the design on the floor; let dry.
- **Use the black marking pen** to add dark details, such as outlines.
- **Use the white acrylic paint** and the #10 flat brush to add light details, including lines on the racetrack.
- **Using the 3-inch flat brush,** apply two or three coats of varnish or acrylic top coat over the designs for protection; let each coat dry before you apply the next.

CUSTOM-COVERED LAMPSHADE
(PROJECT SHOWN ON PAGE 12)

Give a simple lamp a designer look with a custom-covered lampshade.

- **Wrap paper or fabric around** the lampshade and mark the material to indicate the top and bottom edges of the shade. Add ½ inch all around to make a pattern.
- **Cut the paper or fabric** along the marked lines.
- **Center the shade on the cutout** and glue along the top and bottom edges.
- **Turn under the edges** and adhere with hot glue. If your shade is significantly smaller at the top than at the bottom, you'll need to clip excess paper or fabric every ¼ inch and turn the fringed edges to the inside and glue in place. If desired, glue ribbon or braid over the fringed edges for a clean finish and adorn the bottom of the shade with beaded fringe.
- **Glue** ready-made adornments to the lamp base. If desired, paint or decoupage the lamp base to match other accessories in the room.

Caution: Lampshades that sit close to a bulb may get warm when the light is on. Use nonflammable glues and papers that can withstand heat. Don't use low-temperature glue guns, because the glue may soften. Never use a lightbulb with a higher wattage than recommended by the lamp manufacturer.

COLORFUL WINDOW TOPPER

SKILL LEVEL

Intermediate sewer or upholsterer

SUPPLIES

- Iron and ironing board
- 45-inch-wide fabric
- Contrasting fabric ribbon
- Matching threads
- Needle
- Sewing machine capable of making buttonholes
- Sewing scissors
- Staples and staple gun
- 1×4-inch wood board
- L-brackets
- Screws
- Screwdriver
- Measuring tape and ruler
- Chalk
- Hand saw

COLORFUL WINDOW TOPPER
(PROJECT SHOWN ON PAGES 58–59)

This easy-to-make fabric cornice introduces cheerful pattern and color with a minimum of sewing time and fabric yardage.

- **Measure the window width** and add 2 inches.
- **Cut the 1×4-inch board** to this measured length.
- **Cut a length of 45-inch-wide fabric** to equal the width of the window frame plus 20 inches.
- **Fold the fabric in half lengthwise** with right sides facing. Iron in a sharp crease.
- **Stitch the edges together** with a ½-inch seam allowance, leaving an opening for turning. Clip corners, turn right side out, and press. Slip-stitch the opening closed.
- **Fold a box pleat** at the center of the double-sided fabric length: Allow 2 inches in the center, then make 1-inch folds.
- **Press the box pleat** and slip-stitch the folds in place.
- **Using a ruler and chalk,** mark ½-inch vertical slits at 2-inch intervals along each side of the box pleat.
- **Stitch buttonholes** over the marks and slit the buttonholes open.
- **Braid the contrasting fabric ribbon** through the buttonholes as shown *above right*.
- **Using a staple gun,** staple the top of the box pleat to the top center of the precut 1×4-inch board. Then staple the rest of the valance to the top of the board, working out to each end.
- **Wrap the fabric around the ends** of the board.

Staple in place.
- **Trim off** any excess fabric wrap.
- **Mount L-brackets** above the window frame.
- **Attach the covered cornice board** to the L-brackets with screws.

CHENILLE CURTAINS
SKILL LEVEL
Novice sewer
SUPPLIES
- Vintage chenille bedspread
- Bedsheet
- Thread
- Sewing needle
- Fabric scraps
- Felt
- Decorative ribbon
- Double curtain rod
- Buttons
- Scissors
- Sewing machine

PATCHWORK PILLOW
SKILL LEVEL
Novice sewer
SUPPLIES
- Computer and printer
- Patchwork fabric scraps
- Chambray fabric
- Green fabric scraps
- Matching green and dark green thread
- Sewing needle
- Polyester fiberfill
- Pins
- Scissors

CHENILLE CURTAINS
(PROJECT SHOWN ON PAGES 78–79)

A vintage chenille bedspread and a yellow sheet cover this bedroom window with style.

- **To make the panels,** trim the top of the bedspread to the desired length, leaving the fringe as an accent along the bottom and sides.
- **Cut the bedsheet** down the middle and trim raw edges to make two panels the same size as the chenille panels.
- **For each curtain panel,** align finished edges of one sheet panel and one chenille panel with right sides together. Sew along the raw edges; turn right side out.
- **Topstitch the bottom and side edges** of the sheet to form a rod pocket; fold the chenille to just below the rod pocket and topstitch in place.
- **Hang the panels** on the inside of the double curtain rod.
- **To make the flowers,** cut floral shapes from fabric scraps. Sew around the cutout shapes.
- **For the flower centers,** cut a circle from felt. Hand-sew the circle to the flower and stitch a button onto the circle.
- **To hang the flowers** on the outer rod, sew a length of ribbon to each flower to resemble a stem, then tie the completed flowers in place.
- **Hand-sew another piece of ribbon** horizontally along the stem's top edge and again a few inches down the stem to create a rod pocket.
- **Slip the flowers** onto the outer curtain rod.

PATCHWORK PILLOW
(PROJECT SHOWN ON PAGE 79)

A patchwork pillow is a smart way to bring together all the fabrics in your child's room. Adding a favorite phrase or the child's name lets you personalize it even more.

- **To create the words,** use a computer to print out the desired letters; use these as patterns to cut the letters from fabric.
- **Cut as many equal-size fabric squares** as needed for your particular design. Arrange the squares in the desired pattern and hand-sew the letters to the squares. Using ½-inch seam allowances, sew the squares to each other to form the pillow front. From chambray, cut a pillow back the same size as the pillow front.
- **Cut leaves from various green fabric scraps.** Cut a matching top and bottom piece for each leaf.
- **With right sides facing,** stitch the leaves together, leaving an opening at the stem end; turn right side out.
- **Topstitch the leaves with dark green thread** to form veins.
- **Pin a set of three leaves to each corner** of the pillow back. The leaves should be right side up, with the stem end pointing toward the center of the pillow.
- **Pin together the pillow front and back, with right sides facing** and raw edges aligned. Sew, leaving an opening at the bottom for stuffing.
- **Turn right side out,** stuff with fiberfill, and whipstitch the opening closed.

CARDIGAN PILLOW

(PROJECT SHOWN ON PAGE 79)

To make this pretty cardigan sweater pillow, select a sweater your child loves but has outgrown or pick up a gently used sweater at a secondhand store.

- **Button the sweater** and lay flat.
- **Cut off the arms and the top, bottom,** and side edges to make two equal size squares from the sweater back and front.
- **With right sides together,** sew along all four edges.
- **Unbutton the sweater,** turn right side out, and stuff with polyester fiberfill.

PAINTED HEADBOARD

(PROJECT SHOWN ON PAGE 79)

Customize a bed to match your child's room by adding extra color and pattern to a wooden headboard. Here, the entire bed was primed and painted white; then the headboard and footboard were given robin's egg blue and sunshine yellow accents.

- **Sand the headboard and footboard** lightly. Wipe with a lint-free cloth, prime, and let dry.
- **Cover all the surfaces** with two coats of durable white latex enamel paint using the 3-inch flat brush; let dry.
- **Accentuate the headboard and footboard** by painting a favorite accent color within the recessed areas or by repeating the outline of the headboard's or footboard's shape as shown with the 1½-inch tapered brush; let dry.
- **Using two coats of** another favorite accent color and the #10 artist's brush, paint freehand polka dots. For a precise dot, use a circle stencil.

For stenciling advice, see page 117.

BRIGHT PAINTED DRESSER
SKILL LEVEL
Novice painter
SUPPLIES
- Latex primer
- Sandpaper
- Tack cloth
- Latex enamel paint in the desired colors
- Paintbrushes: 3-inch flat and #10 artist's brushes
- Pencil and paper
- Optional: Painter's tape
- Optional: stamps or stencils and acrylic paints in the desired colors
- Polyurethane

BRIGHT PAINTED DRESSER
(PROJECT SHOWN ON PAGE 28)

Enliven a plain dresser with painted designs, including whimsical checks and polka dots. The checks were painted freehand; for a more precise pattern, mask off the stripes before painting. The animals shown on the bottom drawer were hand-painted, but you could also stamp or stencil these designs. This project uses a sturdy, unfinished dresser with wooden pulls, but it is also appropriate for a vintage chest.

- **Remove the drawers from the dresser.** Lightly sand the dresser and drawers; wipe with a tack cloth. Prime all surfaces; let dry.
- **Paint the dresser and drawers** with one color of enamel paint. Paint two coats, letting the paint dry between coats. Plan the freehand designs on paper, sketching your ideas. Determine the width of the checks. Paint the checks, polka dots, and animals using #10 artist's paintbrushes and desired paint colors. Allow the drawers to dry thoroughly.
- **To protect the surface,** seal the dresser and drawers with two coats of polyurethane, allowing time for it to dry between coats.
- **Reinsert the drawers** into the dresser.

PAINTING WOOD FURNITURE

Painted furnishings add charm and personality to a child's room. Customizing a piece of furniture to match any decor is quite easy if you follow these basic guidelines.

- **Select new unfinished or sturdy vintage pieces for your project.** If the piece has been previously painted, in most cases you can sand and repaint without stripping off the old paint.
- **To make a surface ready for painting,** first lightly sand the piece. Wipe with a tack cloth to remove dust. For even coverage, prime the piece with primer tinted the same color as the desired base coat.
- **Select high-quality paints** that will adhere well to the primed surface. In general, latex enamel paints work best for painting furnishings. When applying the paint, use thin, even coats and remember to allow the paint to dry thoroughly between coats.
- **Sealing the completed piece with water-base nonyellowing polyurethane** is always recommended to protect the piece from everyday wear and tear.

PLAID WALLS
SKILL LEVEL

Experienced painter

SUPPLIES

- Latex glaze
- Latex or acrylic paints in the desired colors
- Paintbrush: 1½-inch tapered
- Mixing containers
- Low-tack painter's tape
- Tape measure
- Chalk
- Carpenter's level
- Optional: sea sponge

UPHOLSTERED DESK
SKILL LEVEL

Novice upholsterer

SUPPLIES

- Simply designed, ready-to-assemble desk with optional glass top
- Printed 100-percent cotton fabric
- Sewing scissors
- Staple gun and staples

PLAID WALLS
(PROJECT SHOWN ON PAGES **52** AND **53**)

A combination of 6-inch-wide vertical and horizontal stripes created the plaid pattern on the walls *above*. The stripes form panels slightly wider than the bed. These stripes were painted, but for a fabriclike texture, sponge the glazed stripes onto the walls, then drag a dry household paintbrush across the wet glaze, letting each color dry before applying the next. The panels shown are topped with hand-painted flowers, but you could easily stencil similar designs.

- **Start with freshly painted solid-color walls.** In this bedroom, the walls were painted a medium periwinkle. The plaid pattern shown was made using three colors of vertical stripes (blue, orange, burgundy) and four colors of horizontal rows (peach, green, burgundy, blue). Experiment with colors on scrap paper to create the best color combination for your child's room.
- **To make the pattern,** measure and mask off the the vertical stripes. Paint using the 1½-inch tapered brush and latex or acrylic paints, letting each color dry before applying the next.
- **For the horizontal stripes,** mix the paints with the glaze to create a transparent appearance. **Note:** Different paints require different paint-to-glaze ratios. To ensure satisfactory results, test your colors on a primed piece of foam-core board before applying them to the wall. A 2:1 ratio of paint to glaze was used here.
- **Measure, mask off, and paint** the horizontal stripes.

UPHOLSTERED DESK
(PROJECT SHOWN ON PAGE **55**)

- **Start with a basic desk** or small table that has simple lines. Carved adornments are difficult (and sometimes impossible) to cover. If possible, purchase a ready-to-assemble desk and upholster the pieces prior to assembly. If you use an existing piece, removing the legs and disassembling the remaining portion will simplify the process.
- **If you're new to upholstering,** choose an allover print, such as a floral or polka-dot, in a sturdy 100-percent cotton fabric that does not stretch easily. Stay away from solids, because they will show all mistakes.
- **Lay out the disassembled** desk pieces, experimenting with the fabric to find the most suitable placement.
- **Cut the fabric** to fit the desk pieces, leaving several extra inches on all sides for turning and stapling. For the legs, cut fabric rectangles on the bias (diagonally) to cover the length and circumference of the legs.
- **Starting with one desktop corner,** turn the fabric over and staple it to the bottom of the desk top. Keeping the fabric taut and even, staple the other three desktop corners. Repeat the process for the desk sides, stapling the fabric to the desk bottom.
- **For the legs,** start at the top and hold the fabric taut. Staple the fabric in place with seams on back edge.

PAINTED STARS AND GALAXIES

SKILL LEVEL
Novice painter

SUPPLIES
- Star template, copied into several different sizes
- Galaxy template, copied into several different sizes
- Clear acetate sheets
- Fine-tip marker
- Crafts or utility knife with spare blades
- Cutting mat
- Latex paint: midnight blue
- Sparkling white stenciling cream
- Stenciling brushes
- Paintbrush: 3-inch flat
- Sea sponge

PAINTED STARS AND GALAXIES
(PROJECT SHOWN ON PAGE 77)
- **To create stencils** from the templates, use a copy machine to enlarge or reduce the patterns as desired.
- **Place the clear acetate** over the star and galaxy copies. Trace the outline onto the acetate using a fine-tip marker.
- **Working on a cutting mat,** cut out the stencil designs with a crafts or utility knife. Have plenty of extra blades on hand so you can switch to a sharper one whenever necessary.
- **To create a wall treatment** similar to this one, paint the walls with two or more coats of midnight blue paint until you achieve a uniform look; let dry thoroughly.
- **Using sparkling white** acrylic stenciling cream and a stenciling brush, stencil stars of varying sizes onto the wall in a random fashion or create constellations.
- **While the stenciled stars are still wet,** use a damp sea sponge to soften the edges, creating a glowing halo-like effect, as shown in the photographs *top left* and *top right.*
- **Repeat the stenciling process** with the galaxy stencils.

Note: For more information on creating custom stencils and basic stenciling techniques, see page 117.

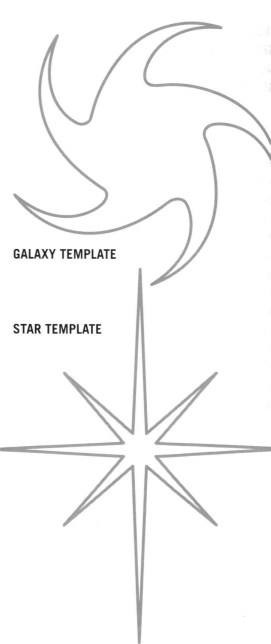

GALAXY TEMPLATE

STAR TEMPLATE

FLOORCLOTH FOCUS

SKILL LEVEL

Novice painter

SUPPLIES

• Linoleum remnant

• Latex primer

• Latex paint in the desired colors

• Scissors or crafts knife

• Paintbrushes: 3-inch flat and 1½-inch tapered; #10 flat artist's brush

• Acrylic paint in the desired color

• Black permanent marking pen

• Pencil and paper

• Satin-finish interior varnish

FLOORCLOTH FOCUS

(**PROJECT SHOWN ON PAGE** 107)

Colorful and easy to make, painted linoleum floorcloths protect the floor from spills and drips and brighten any decor. Here, the back side of a linoleum remnant becomes the front side of the painted floorcloth. If you cannot find a suitable remnant, look for specially designed floorcloth canvases at crafts and art supply stores. If your child would prefer a shape other than an octopus, the following instructions will still serve as a guide.

■ **Sketch the desired shape onto paper.** Enlarge as desired and trace onto the front of the linoleum remnant. If you are confident of your drawing abilities, sketch the design directly onto the linoleum.

■ **Cut out the shape with scissors or a crafts knife,** taking care to make smooth cuts.

■ **Using the 3-inch flat paintbrush,** prime the back of the linoleum shape; let dry.

■ **Paint the back of the linoleum shape** with two coats of one color latex paint; let dry after each coat.

■ **Pencil tentacles, eyes, and mouth** onto the painted linoleum piece. Trace over the penciled lines with a black marking pen; let dry.

■ **Using the #10 flat brush** for edges and a 1½-inch tapered brush for interiors, paint the spaces between the tentacles with another color of latex paint; let dry.

■ **Using the #10 flat brush,** paint the eyes with the acrylic paint; let dry. Add black pupils with

the marking pen; let dry.

■ **Using the 3-inch flat brush,** apply two coats of varnish; let dry between coats.

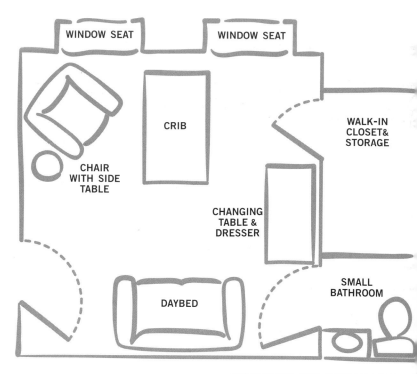

WINDOW SEAT WINDOW SEAT

CRIB

WALK-IN CLOSET & STORAGE

CHAIR WITH SIDE TABLE

CHANGING TABLE & DRESSER

DAYBED

SMALL BATHROOM

NURSERIES AND TODDLER ROOMS

SUCCESSFUL ROOM ARRANGEMENTS

Regardless of your child's age, choosing an arrangement that is safe and functional is a priority. Whether your child has his or her own space or shares a room with a sibling, the following information will help you plan a room that you can all be comfortable with.

Nurseries and Toddler Rooms

Room arrangements play a large part in keeping your infant safe and comfortable. The center of the room is an ideal spot for a crib; it keeps your infant away from potentially dangerous window treatment cords and safe from drafts that occur near windows and heating and cooling vents. This plan also frees up wall space for dressers, changing tables, and comfy reading and rocking chairs; you may even have room for a daybed for nights when baby doesn't want to be alone.

As your child grows, he or she can move to the daybed, and the crib can be moved out of the room altogether, making room for a play table or a comfy rug and floor pillows.

Grade-School Rooms

If you have an elementary-age child, consider arranging his or her room in activity zones, as shown on pages 66–69. That room is divided into four functional sections: a write and think

station, sleep and dream chamber, create and play area, and read and relax haven. Create zones that suit the activities your child is most involved with, such as practicing dance moves, playing an instrument, or dribbling a basketball or soccer ball.

Sharing During the Grade-School Years

Shared rooms designed for 6- to 11-year-olds need to provide privacy and storage space.

- **For more privacy,** the beds are moved to opposite sides of the room and are on different levels. One is a loft-style bed.
- **A dresser fits under the loft** for additional storage. Small storage units double as bedside tables for the other twin bed.
- **For hobbies and projects** done together or individually, a colorful table and chairs offer plenty of space.
- **Storage by the table** holds art supplies, books, and other materials for this activity and homework area.

Sharing During the Teen Years

As sibling roommates edge into their teens, their room needs to work even harder: Privacy and expanded study space are essential. Rearranging some of the furniture can transform the space so it can accommodate new pursuits.

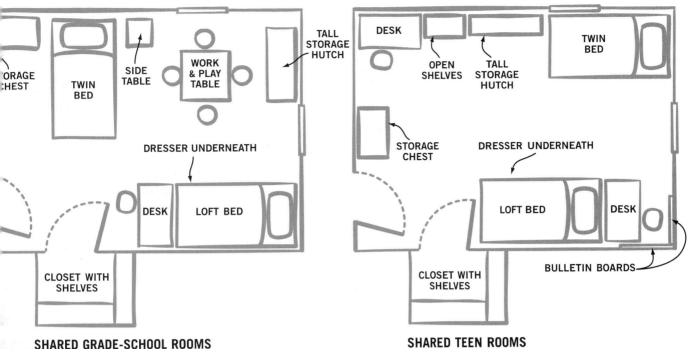

SHARED GRADE-SCHOOL ROOMS

(Diagram labels: STORAGE CHEST, TWIN BED, SIDE TABLE, WORK & PLAY TABLE, TALL STORAGE HUTCH, DRESSER UNDERNEATH, DESK, LOFT BED, CLOSET WITH SHELVES)

SHARED TEEN ROOMS

(Diagram labels: DESK, OPEN SHELVES, TALL STORAGE HUTCH, TWIN BED, STORAGE CHEST, DRESSER UNDERNEATH, LOFT BED, DESK, CLOSET WITH SHELVES, BULLETIN BOARDS)

- **To create separate study areas** and minimize distractions, the beds are moved so there's private space at opposite ends of the room.
- **The desk at the end of the loft bed** has storage beneath the bed and a corner bulletin board. Expanded vertical shelving surrounds the other desk, providing shared library space.
- **The table and chairs** are eliminated to make room for the new bed arrangement.
- **Lively colors** in the furnishings, floor covering, and bed linens are pleasing to teens and younger children, so the palette stays the same.

Peaceful Divisions

Dividing one space into two cozy domains doesn't require costly remodeling, but it does take creativity. As you plan room arrangements, brainstorm with your children and incorporate their ideas and needs. Ideally, the dividers you choose will be flexible enough to meet changing needs for shared time and privacy. Check that dividers allow adequate heat, air, and light to reach both sides of the room. These items help divide a space:

- **Modular, stackable bookcases.**
- **A large chalkboard** on casters.
- **A row of low storage units,** such as plastic bins or cubes, lined up across the floor.
- **A shelving unit,** with shelves on both sides,

that stretches from the floor to the ceiling.
- **A two-sided storage unit** with closed and see-through shelving.
- **A whole wall or half-wall** made from wallboard.
- **Well-attached, ceiling-mounted blinds** or curtain panels; these are safer than floor screens, which can topple over.

For the Teenager

Letting teens arrange their furniture is an easy way to give them some freedom and independence. If your teen isn't interested in helping with furniture arrangement, arrange the pieces so there is easy access to storage drawers and closets (so your teen might actually use them). Allow adequate space for friends to gather and hang out. Move the bed far enough away from the wall so that making it requires little effort. Choose linens and comforters that are lightweight and easy to toss over sheets and pillows.

index

RESOURCES
Design Resources

U.S. UNITS TO METRIC EQUIVALEN		
To Convert From	Multiply By	To Get
Inches	25.4	Millimeters
Inches	2.54	Centimeter
Feet	30.48	Centimeter
Feet	0.3048	Meters (m)

METRIC UNITS TO U.S. EQUIVALEN		
To Convert From	Multiply By	To Get
Millimeters	0.0394	Inches
Centimeters	0.3937	Inches
Centimeters	0.0328	Feet
Meters	3.2808	Feet